Is Mise
I am Cara

Is Mise Cara / I am Cara

Orbs, Souls and Holy Ghosts

Dr Kieran Mervyn
Faye Mervyn

COPYRIGHT

ISBN 9781800491496

Publisher: Independent Publishing Network.
Publication date: 2020
Authors: Dr. Kieran Mervyn. Faye Mervyn.
Email: ismisecara@gmail.com
Address: 6 Bedford Mount, Cookridge, Leeds. LS16 6DP, UK.
Website: www.ismisecara.com
Please direct all enquiries to the authors.

For Finn and his 'Guardian Angel', Cara

ACKNOWLEDGMENTS

Writing a book about our beautiful daughter was more challenging than we anticipated but more rewarding than we could have imagined. We must start by thanking a special lady – the spiritual messenger, Lorna Byrne, and her daughter Pearl. From reading early drafts to giving us advice on copyright and guiding us spiritually through the tough times, we could not have done it without you. Thank you so much. We are eternally grateful to our old friend and mentor, Terry Boyle (RIP). A fantastic character who provided magic to our book through his editing and constant guidance. To Cara's Grandparents, Paddy and Marie, David and Hazel and Cara's Aunties, Uncles and Cousins for all the love and support. Many thanks to Khalid to Yasemin Mukhtar and family for their compassion since Cara passed. To Father Emmanuel for his role in Cara's life, overseeing the funeral and helping us to navigate through the follow-up events. To everyone who donated to the Yorkshire Brain Tumour Research and Support charity at the funeral and afterwards via Jennie Castlehouse's pending London Marathon in 2021. We are forever grateful to everyone who cared for Cara at the Leeds General Infirmary, St James' Hospital, and respite centre. THANK YOU to the NHS – for supporting Cara through almost twelve years of life. Special thanks to all of Cara's schoolteachers and friends, especially Sarah-Jane and Philip and their families. To Ray and Mena Brennan and family for being there, and a particular thanks to Ray and son, Pierce for creating the beautiful book cover. And thanks to Harigo, Ben, Rohan, staff, friends and colleagues from Leeds University, Leeds Beckett University, London South Bank University (Health Systems Innovation Lab) and the University of Roehampton, London. A special thanks to Our Lord, Mary Queen of the Gael, and the Angels. May this book provide HOPE to those who wish to understand more about supernatural and paranormal experiences, especially at a time of grief. It is what Cara would have wanted.

Contents

COPYRIGHT   IV

ACKNOWLEDGMENTS   6

PREFACE   3

CHAPTER 1 ~ WHO IS CARA?   1

MAGOO ARRIVES   3
RELEASE FROM NEONATAL   11
ANOTHER INTUBATION   17
LITTLE BOY PASSES AWAY   23
BACK HOME   27
SURGERY: SUMMER OF 2009   33
FIRST TRIP TO IRELAND   39
TRIAL WARD DECANNULATION   41
TANZANIAN IRISH WEDDING   47
SURGERY AFTER STARTING SCHOOL   50
LITTLE GIRL FROM BRADFORD   57
CARA'S BREATHING EXERCISES   63
FIRST NEW YEARS IN BELFAST   67
BIG SISTER CARA   69
CHRISTENING BEFORE HOUSE MOVE   75
BRAINSTEM TUMOUR DIAGNOSIS   77
KNARESBOROUGH   83
WATERBABY   87
MAKING THE MOST OF LIFE   89
DONEGAL FAMILY HOLIDAY   93
TURF LODGE FAITH HEALER   97
MRI SCANS   99
CARDINAL HEENAN HIGH SCHOOL   105
CARA'S LAST CHRISTMAS   107
CARA'S LAST MEAL   111
NOTE FROM UNCLE DAMIEN   115

CHAPTER 2 ~ BLACK IS THE COLOUR   119

BLACK IS THE COLOUR: 'CARA'S SONG'   119
OUR VERY OWN ANGEL?   123
SPIORAID NAOIMH: HOLY GHOSTS   125

MUM'S DREAM   129
CARA'S FUNERAL   131
CARA'S OBITUARY   135
PAULINE'S AFTER THE FUNERAL   141
THE ROOM IS BUZZING   143
DONEGAL PLAQUE   147
ASHES AND THE EMERALD ANGEL   149
TAKING ASHES TO BELFAST   151
CHILD: BELFAST AIRPORT   153

CHAPTER 3 ~ SENSE MAKING   **157**

CARA'S ALL AROUND?   157
CORONERS LETTER   161
VISION OF CHILD AND GIRL   165
GIRL WITH THE LONG DARK HAIR   167
THE GOD SPOT   169
REACHING OUT TO LORNA BYRNE   173
LORNA DELIVERS A MESSAGE FROM CARA   179
RED ORBS ARE CIRCLING   185
LET THE HEALING BEGIN   187
CARA APPEARS TO GRANNY MARIE   193
POST-MORTEM FOLLOW-UP RESULTS   195
KHALID'S VISION   197
SEEKING ALTERNATIVE PERSPECTIVES   201
CHINESE FARMER   209
TELEPATHIC 'DREAMS'   212
THE EXORCISM   223
TERRY BOYLE (RIP)   227
LORNA BYRNE'S SECOND MEETING   231
KIERAN: MAKING SENSE OF IT ALL   238
CONCLUSION AND A LETTER TO CARA   241

ABOUT THE AUTHORS   **244**

KIERAN'S PUBLICATIONS   **245**

QUOTE IN MEMORY OF "MAGOO"   **247**

BIBLIOGRAPHY   **248**

PREFACE

This book emerged soon after the death of our beautiful 11-year-old daughter, Cara Mia Mervyn (RIP - 12.2.2008 - 29.12.2019). Is mise Cara (Irish Gaelic for 'I am Cara') includes a website www.ismisecara.com, dedicated to our precious girl. The book rekindles memories of her life but also carries a broader message from the spirit world. In the poetic words of Mary Elizabeth Frye (1):

> *Do not stand at my grave and weep.*
> *I am not there; I do not sleep.*
> *I am a thousand winds that blow,*
> *I am the diamond glint on snow.*
> *I am the sunlight on ripened grain,*
> *I am the gentle autumn rain.*
> *When you wake in the morning hush,*
> *I am the swift, uplifting rush.*
> *Of quiet birds in circling flight,*
> *I am the soft starlight at night.*
> *Do not stand at my grave and weep,*
> *I am not there; I do not sleep.*
> *(Do not stand at my grave and cry.*
> *I am not there; I did not die!)*

Do Not Stand at My Grave and Weep

Cara's funeral mass was held on January 16th, 2020. The priest (Father Emmanuel from the Holy Name of Jesus Catholic Church in Leeds) told the 2000-year-old fable of a Chinese farmer (2). This story perfectly summed up Cara's life and afterlife.

A Chinese farmer gets a horse, which soon runs away. A neighbour says, "That's bad news." The farmer replies, "Good news, bad news, who can say?" The horse comes back and brings another horse with him. Good news, you might say. The farmer gives the second horse to his son, who rides it, then is thrown and badly breaks his leg. "So sorry for your bad news," says the concerned neighbour. "Good news, bad news, who can say?" the farmer replies. In a week or so, the emperor's men come and take every able-bodied young man to fight in a war. The farmer's son is spared. Good news, of course.

The Taoist theology inspired story of the Chinese farmer resonates with our recent experiences. The tale has encouraged us to take a philosophical look at events since Cara died. It is difficult not to get too attached, e.g. to thoughts of 'what if' what if we had checked on Cara at three am after hearing a noise from her bedroom? Or, what if we had taken her to hospital earlier that night?

I was glad to speak to a colleague from Leeds University (Dr Alistair Norman) who advised me not to blame myself for failing to investigate the noise that night. How we had supported Cara immensely through the years and that it was sadly just her time to go.

Writing this book has been mentally exhausting, but also surprisingly therapeutic. We now hope to create a legacy for Cara by helping others through messages of hope.

Chapter 1 ~ Who is Cara?

In Irish Gaelic, the word Cara means a dear friend. It overlaps with other forms such as 'beloved' in Latin; 'expensive' or 'face' in Spanish and a 'diamond' in Vietnamese. CARA is a service based out of The Leeds Irish Centre that supports people with complex needs. It is also involved in locating and engaging with older people who have lost touch with family. CARA helps people to reconnect and feel part of an extensive support network.

So, the Leeds Irish connection with the historical name 'Cara' seemed a perfect fit. And as you will see, Cara was true to her name. She became incredibly passionate about the socially excluded, whether giving money or food to the homeless or buying products to support refugees. We were delighted when her picture drew first prize in a luxurious hamper competition at Trinity Leeds Shopping Centre in support of Syrian refugees, just before Christmas 2014. Her drawing in primary school was also chosen by National Rail in their 'Safety on the Tracks' initiative.

Cara would often ask us to play songs such as 'Missing You' (3)(about dislocated Irish people in England) as we drove around Leeds.

Where the Summer is Fine, but the Winter's a Fridge.
Wrapped Up in Old Cardboard Under Charing Cross Bridge
And I'll Never Go Home Now Because of the Shame.
Of Misfit's Reflection in a Shop Windowpane
(**Excerpts From 'Missing You' by Christy Moore**).

The first part of the book describes Cara's life growing up in Leeds amidst the various health challenges from premature birth through to death on December 29th, 2019.

It then takes the reader on a mystical journey by relaying supernatural and paranormal experiences since Cara died, before attempting to interpret their meaning in the context of global events.

Father Emmanuel, who knew Cara and Finn (Cara's brother) personally, visited us to discuss a mysterious phenomenon that we had started to experience, before and after the funeral.

After listening carefully and offering a blessing, he advised us to share these stories wisely; to avoid preaching or trying to convert people.

As a result, we encourage you, the reader, to keep an open mind. We take great courage in the visions, visitations, and the orbs (our new reality) but acknowledge that the picture is not perfect or rosy. We share a myriad of conscious, real-life experiences mixed with vivid dreams – some of which seem to interconnect.

The internationally renowned author, Lorna Byrne, kindly took time out of her busy schedule to engage with us and thus plays a central role in the book.

Something BIG happened the day that Cara died, and a window has opened which provides us with a glimpse into the spirit world. Darker forces often accompany the exquisiteness that surrounds us. Still, our faith simultaneously gives us the courage, insight and strength when needed when dealing with grief.

Magoo Arrives

It was the Manchester United v. Manchester City derby. The plan was to visit Bradford for an Indian meal before finding somewhere to watch the match. Bradford was a much safer bet for a United supporter to cheer the team. Faye's dad David arrived mid-morning to take me on a driving lesson around Horsforth and Yeadon while Faye soaked in a hot bath.

David needed the patience of a saint when teaching me to drive along the winding roads of Leeds Bradford Airport in our 1992 Fiat motor. Curries were off the menu for a large part of Faye's pregnancy, until now, as strange cravings took over.

After the driving lesson, I entered the living room and noticed how Faye seemed to be struggling. Holding her stomach, she complained about a dull and heavy ache, so I immediately called the midwife for advice before driving to the Leeds General Infirmary (LGI) hospital. Faye was quickly checked over, diagnosed with a potential UTI, and then discharged.

We went home to watch the match and decided to order a takeaway pizza. Things quickly deteriorated at home. An ambulance arrived as the pizza delivery driver rapped the door. It was pandemonium, as Faye was wheeled into the ambulance and rushed to the hospital for assessments and drops of blood in A&E. She fainted before being transferred to the maternity unit.

3

The next morning, Faye was 2cm dilated. Things were not looking good, and there was a strong possibility that the baby would arrive around 9pm that evening. We both just looked at each other in shock. The doctor decided to inject Faye with steroids to protect the baby's lungs and increase its chances of survival. Two doses, twelve hours apart.

That morning, David arrived in Barcelona for a business meeting. Just before unpacking, Faye's mum Hazel rang him to explain that things were more severe than had initially been thought. Faye's sister Lucy had come down to support us during the labour as the clock ticked towards 9pm.

We rang the priest that afternoon from a darkened labour room. He told us over the phone's loudspeaker how we would always be the child's parents no matter what happens before all four of us prayed together. Shortly afterwards, there was a sense of joy that they had managed to delay the labour and provide precious time for an injection of the second set of steroids.

Lucy returned home for food and rest, and we managed a quick nap. Faye organised a side bed for me after previously sleeping on two blue hardback hospital armchairs. Early the next morning, the new midwife introduced herself. She seemed quite happy with Faye's progress and left to assist two other births.

Still, shortly afterwards, the pain became intense and continued until Faye was in agony. Just then, Faye's mum and dad rang to say that they were on route to the hospital. David managed to rush back from Spain. Once they arrived, their visit enabled me to return home for a bath and change of clothes.

While I was away, one of the doctors visited Faye and wondered if it was a kidney problem and quickly arranged a scan. The midwife had been counting the contractions and sought a second opinion as it may have been a sign of full labour. A second doctor checked and confirmed that Faye was now fully dilated and ready to give birth.

David agreed to call me if there was any change. Once I got home, I went straight to the fridge, which consisted of milk, cheese, and a carton of mushrooms because we had not done our weekly shopping. With dazed eyes, I washed and cut the mushrooms and fried them in olive oil and garlic.

So hungry; I ate them in seconds but remembered how bitter they tasted. I climbed into an uncomfortably lukewarm bath on a cold February day, and remember thinking, 'it's a cert that our phone rings'. About 30 seconds later, it rang – almost screeching at me. I piled out of the bath, dripping wet and shivering with fear, and will never forget David's words: 'Kieran – get down here now'.

Within minutes, I found myself running about the house in a panic, half-praying and half-crying while trying to collect pyjamas and other things on Faye's list for the hospital. I tripped over the Molly Malone statue on top of the stairs, and her head flew off. It sat headless for weeks afterwards until we eventually binned it. I then phoned a taxi, and my heart sank as my wallet contained only £1.30 in loose change.

Luckily, he was a gentleman, telling me to forget about the money and to sit tight. He must have been doing 70mph through the narrow back streets of Bramley, past Armley prison and down Stanningley road and onto the hospital forecourt.

Once I arrived, Hazel accompanied Faye and appeared calm as she explained what was happening. She described me storming in 'like a water buffalo' and spent more time trying to calm me down as Faye squirmed with pain beside us. Faye jokes that a neutral observer would have been thinking that it was me in labour.

The Consultant informed us that it was 50/50 whether the child would make it, which sent a chill through our bones. But I remember thinking that we have still got a chance - a fighting chance.

That is when reality kicked home. Things proceeded quickly as gas and air were replaced by the time to 'PUSH'.

I left the room for a breather and noticed David had his hands fixed on the walls outside the delivery room and seemed to be praying. Faye's gasps became more prevalent as she pushed with all her might. Finally, the medical staff, including three doctors and another midwife, took over and worked carefully to deliver Cara.

Within seconds, our baby had arrived. The midwife advised us to listen for a cry because 'it's a sign the baby had made it'. She seemed to pause for a few seconds before letting out an almighty squeal.

We were in tears as our first-born arrived, as I shouted, "It's a BOY, Faye, it's a wee boy", before one of the midwives looked at me bemused, pointedly telling me that it was a 'little girl'.

The umbilical cord threw me, and the team had a good laugh at my expense. We all needed a laugh at that time. We remember feeling on top of the world.

Cara's big eyes and infectious smile, led us to nickname her 'Magoo'. We briefly stroked her face but were not allowed a cuddle as the clinicians quickly took over.

She was dressed in a small yellow woollen hat and snuggled in a white blanket.

After transfer to the neonatal intensive care unit, we called family and friends and shared the good news.

Faye went to rest as I strolled over to the Joseph Wells bar adjacent to the hospital for a celebratory pint of Guinness.

I remember standing outside and feeling guilty about leaving them both. So, I changed my mind about the drink and went on a mission to find Cara.

Upon entering the neonatal unit, I remember seeing some empty incubators before spotting what resembled a little doll at the far side. She looked smaller and more fragile compared to earlier.

Sleeping soundly, with arms and legs fastened to the mattress, I realised that Cara had a long way to go. Her micro size and shape paled in significance to my nieces, some of whom resembled baby giants when born.

Cara's arrival felt like a gift from God, and we were prepared for whatever, so long as she survived.

Shortly afterwards, the doctor informed us about the decision to transfer Cara to St James's (Jimmy's) University Hospital because of a lack of space at the LGI.

We visited Cara every day - often twice a day to do her cares. Our tasks included cleaning and changing her baby grow inside the incubator, which was fun and games.

The neonatal unit was a hive of energy, but the beeping machines and crying babies were overwhelming. We quickly realised the significance of having a premature child.

The nursing staff advised us to prepare for a roller coaster experience, and they were not joking. On one occasion during nappy changing, Cara relieved herself, and it projected across the incubator and almost destroyed the side of the glass shield.

She was so fragile that we were terrified of holding her, never mind cleaning and changing nappies.

The transition of watching Cara grow week-by-week felt like we were given a precious challenge – one with incredible potential but laced with uncertainties. The staff and other parents seemed to be experts at everything. Faye describe it like being 'under a microscope' as the nursing staff gradually emphasised our responsibilities.

Until then, we had lived a pretty care-free life, travelling the world as any young couple do, working in countries including Spain, the States and South Korea.

Cara had a cheeky grin and a beautiful smile. After approximately five weeks of continuous, twice-daily visits, we realised that St Patrick's Day was approaching. Jimmy's hospital backs onto Sheepscar and Burmantofts area, with its significant Irish population. We decided to visit Cara earlier that day for cares and cuddles before going out for a few hours in the afternoon.

I bought an Irish rugby shirt for Cara, thinking that it would fit. When I asked the Scottish nurse with wild red hair to help us to dress Cara for pictures, she looked confused and gave me grief for buying the wrong shirt size.

I picked a 2-year-old toddler size instead of a minus two months size for our little mite.

There were plenty of jokes but also some beautiful pictures of Cara on her first St Patrick's Day, with a tiny head and feet peeping from a massively oversized shirt.

Later, we strolled into Sheepscar and could hear the live Irish traditional music from The Harp Pub. The place was small and cosy but heaving with people decked out in Irish regalia.

The live band had the electric presence of the Pogues, and the patrons were legless but having a great time.

The barman from Donegal poured us ice-cold pints of Guinness, and we raised a toast to Cara – our little Leeds Irish princess. We then bid our dues and headed onto Maguires, a much larger Irish pub on Regent Street.

As usual, the live music was fantastic with a brilliant atmosphere. Real characters ran the Regent. 'The Dubliner' looking types with proper beards and purveyors of fine whiskey, or 'Uisce Beatha' as we call it in Ireland – the water of life.

Both establishments have unfortunately closed along with The Pointers. Aware of the need for a clear mind the next morning, we decided to leave for an Indian meal.

After some fish curry and chicken handi, we returned to Bramley for a good night's sleep in preparation for an early start with Cara.

Release from Neonatal

We will always treasure Cara's release from Jimmy's neonatal unit after ten difficult weeks. I parked our new blue Ford Fiesta outside and waited for Faye and the nurse to emerge with Cara. After fastening her in and packing bags into the boot, we went home to adjust to family life with our first-born child.

I remember bringing her upstairs and placing the car seat next to her Moses basket. Within minutes, she was crying her eyes out. We just looked at each other in shock. Being home was completely different from the hemmed-in neonatal room. We went into auto mode and quickly organised the nappies, milk, and feed.

The next two weeks were a complete blur, with nights merging into days. Six or seven weeks in, we noticed Cara's breathing became distorted on our walk to Bramley Shopping Centre. Stopping to check, we decided to take her to the emergency doctors at Lexicon House. Immediately upon arrival, the doctor asked us to lift her from the car seat and confirmed that she was struggling with Croup. The doctor called for an ambulance to whisk Cara back to Jimmy's. I followed behind in the car.

After a few days of oxygen, she seemed to improve and was released home. We were delighted and looked forward to getting home for a bath, a takeaway and a good night's rest after some sleepless nights.

11

At home, we managed to get Cara off to sleep but knew that something was not right. An ambulance arrived within minutes and directed her back to Jimmy's and the clinicians who were familiar with her. I sat next to Cara in the ambulance.

Upon arrival, Cara was placed in a room next to the nurse's desk for close observation. Another sleepless night then ensued as Cara was struggling, even with oxygen.

Early am, the doctors took Cara to a side room, and it required a small team to hold her still as they attempted to embed a cannula.

She fought with every sinew to resist the doctor's needle over an extended period. The relief was palpable when the Consultant found a suitable vein. Once again, I felt that we might lose her.

Faye arrived that Sunday morning (Fathers Day, 2008), enabling me to drive home for a shower and change of clothes before returning. By this time, she seemed to have settled slightly.

The doctors seemed happy enough as she stabilised, advising me to return home to rest while Faye stayed overnight. That evening, as Cara was dozing, the oxygen saturation (O2 sat) monitor started to beep more frequently.

The ward sister decided to call for a doctor. After checking her blood gases, they realised that things were spiralling out of control.

Faye accompanied the sister and doctor as they took Cara up the lift to the paediatric intensive care unit (PICU). It all seemed very controlled and organised.

Once ventilated, Faye called me early that morning to explain the run of events. I arrived that morning feeling dejected and took a wrong turn, walking through the children's cancer unit. It was sad to see the faces of many distressed kids. A nurse then approached and directed me through the oncology unit as a one-off after explaining the situation with Cara.

The whole experience of PICU was like neonatal but on another level. We were informed that she would spend a few days ventilated as a precaution.

The next step would be to remove her from the ventilator tube or take a different route. We walked around Leeds in a daze, going back and forth to PICU but realised that there was nothing to do except put our faith in the Man above.

We both caught up on sleep on the Monday and Tuesday nights before returning on Wednesday morning for a meeting with the PICU doctors.

They explained the plan, which was to take her off the ventilator on Thursday lunchtime but could not guarantee the outcome. One doctor advised that Cara might continue to have stridor, a high-pitched, wheezing sound caused by a disrupted airflow.

There was no guarantee that Cara would survive, but he suggested that girls were much more robust and had a God-given strength. Research evidence shows that it may be down to the childbearing ability of women which enables them to withstand significant discomfort.

That Thursday morning, on route to Jimmy's, we stopped at church for a quick prayer. We found the main door locked and continued onto the hospital.

Upon arrival, I went through to reception and then into a side room to meet with the Consultants and medical doctors. Faye went into a little side room next to PICU because she was experiencing common cold symptoms. She opened her purse, and at the back pocket, noticed a Padre Pio card and began to pray.

The meeting was quick, and the doctor informed me that decannulation was successful. I was buzzing and rushed to tell Faye. After explaining the cold symptoms, the doctors were not concerned and were happy for us to have a quick cuddle with Cara who surprisingly looked well. We now call Cara an enigma, because she often looked radiant and beautiful, even when at death's door. She was our little angel.

The following morning, Cara returned to the ward. That Saturday, my parents Marie and Paddy and sister Sarah and husband Gerry arrived from Belfast and headed straight for Jimmy's. They finally met Cara for the first time. Faye's folks came down and joined us in a family get-together on Sunday afternoon. Next day, after saying our goodbyes to the family, we had a meeting with the hospital Consultants who this time looked stern and uneasy.

They suggested that Cara should not have needed ventilation for Croup and decided to check for an airway problem. Jimmy's then became our home for the next week where the doctors performed further tests.

After a week of careful observations, the ENT surgeon undertook a scope of Cara's airway. To our relief, he found the airway slightly small, but nothing untoward. Again, we were really chuffed to hear the news of Cara's discharge.

The weather was changing. We were adapting better to family life, and grateful that God had answered our prayers. Our wee Magoo was finally coming home. Now, the three of us could plan a summer of activities for the first time.

Our travel options for the summer of 2008 were limited. Being born so early restricted the things that we could plan and do as a family. A summer holiday abroad was a no-go. I decided to put my PhD on hold, but thankfully I had already collected most of the research data.

We implemented a little routine and after a while, were comfortable venturing for short day trips. At that time, we lived in Poplar Rise in Bramley and had easy rail and bus transport to Leeds and Bradford City Centre. Bradford often gets bad press in the media.

To us, on a low budget, it was a little food haven for days out. After loading the pushchair with milk, bottles, and Cara's change bag, the search was on for the best curry houses.

In nice weather, we visited the various restaurants for starters and a quick curry. The Victoria line took us across to Hebden Bridge which was a hippy village leading onto the Pennines.

We would walk the legs off ourselves, stopping to feed Cara and making the most of a day out. Sometimes in Bradford, it was good to venture a bit further towards Westgate and Lumb Lane. Two of our regular spots were the old K2 restaurant and the Sweet Centre. K2 restaurant closed in 2013.

On one visit, the owner introduced himself and recommended the restaurant's signature dish, a staff handi. Handi's are vessels of different curries prepared each day. Monday might be a handi biryani; Wednesday, a fish, goat, chicken or vegetarian dall.

Just when the food arrived, Cara woke in a tizz. Hands outstretched; the owner offered to lift her while telling us about his 'team of grandkids'.

Gesturing for us to enjoy the food, he strolled around the restaurant with Magoo who was loving the attention, carried between customers' tables through to the kitchen window. The chefs were waving and having some banter.

Over the years, Cara quickly became accustomed to the sights and smells of curries and converted into a real foodie. Starting with soft boiled rice, she moved onto chapati, tarka dahl, korma curries and other mild dishes, finished off with locally sourced pistachio ice cream.

Cara developed an appetite to complement her knowledge of food. Her mum spoilt her with great meals and treats, but she would roll her eyes and laugh when news broke that I was cooking.

She knew my penchant for chillies and panicked when I served food, but it was great to see her big smile when I got it right.

Another Intubation

After our summer trips around Bradford and Hebden Bridge, the summer slowly disappeared, and the autumn kicked in with a vengeance. It was brutally cold weather, and we noticed that Cara did not seem 100%. It was a Sunday night when stridor started. She tugged around the neck area, struggling for a breath.

We attended A&E and explained Cara's history and previous problems at Jimmy's hospital back in June 2008. The doctor admitted Cara because of her previous need for ventilation coupled with the current breathing problems.

She remained there for the next four days because of a drop in her oxygen saturation (O2 sat) levels.

By Friday, the saturation levels had improved, and the doctors released her. Occasionally, patients presenting with significant breathing problems are unable to sense their low oxygen levels until it is too late. These patients tend to be intubated and rarely survive.

We were due to fly to Ireland shortly after Cara's release. However, the doctors asked us to sign a form to agree 'not' to travel for Cara's pending christening at St Paul's Chapel in Belfast, because of the risks involved. After taking her home, we got her bathed, fed, and ready for bed.

But our hearts were in our mouths because of Cara's noisy breathing, so we took her straight back down to A&E early that morning. The doctor who had been looking after Cara previously on the ward looked concerned and agreed to keep her in for observation.

After being readmitted, she quickly started to 'desaturate'. Her oxygen levels were low, fluctuating between 70 to low 90% when anything below 95% is a problem.

That Sunday, we took a short break from the hospital and quickly returned after lunch.

Upon entering the ward, we heard a loud rattle. One of the trainee nurses had put Cara in a pushchair for close observation, but Cara's breathing had deteriorated.

We dressed her in comfy pyjamas and gave her some food. She seemed to settle, but we noticed how her neck tugged as she grew increasingly distressed.

The next hour or so became a daze as the doctor returned and checked her oxygen levels and heart rate before calling for a PICU doctor. He soon arrived and took blood samples to check blood gas levels. It took a team of us to hold her down.

'A Blood Gas is a test that helps determine respiratory function, particularly how well a child's body is exchanging Oxygen and Carbon Dioxide, as well as the Acid/base Status (Ph) of the blood. While most commonly used to determine a child's respiratory status, Blood Gases can also assess issues caused by metabolic or renal disorders' (4).

Cara's heart rate was now significantly elevated while her oxygen levels plummeted. The Consultant advised us to expect a tough night. After being rushed to PICU, we waited patiently in the ward for the blood gas results to arrive.

Things happened so quickly that we felt overwhelmed and frightened at the thought of losing Cara. We rang our families before packing some of her baby grows, and cardigans then headed to PICU before being ushered into a side room. Soon afterwards, the nurse called us inside.

The Australian doctor who had previously ventilated Cara back in June was standing next to her bed with a multi-disciplinary team of clinicians. Looking bemused, he shook his head – telling us how fortunate Cara was to be surrounded by medical staff on both occasions.

Serious trouble was looming, and it would have been a disaster without being in proximity to medical expertise. Another doctor who had previously cared for Cara hugged us both before sending us home to rest because apparently, 'we'd need it'.

We drove home and managed a few hours of broken sleep. The next morning on PICU, Cara's nurse asked if we were aware of the next step? Our hearts sank as we learned of their plans to fit a Tracheostomy tube. When the team arrived, a female doctor with a Newcastle accent informed us that this was '100 times worse' compared to the last time that she had intubated Cara. Now she was intubated with a size 2mm 'Endotracheal Tracheal Tube'.

This item is suited to the tiniest of premature babies and apparently no longer available for use in certain hospitals. They range from 2.0 to 5.5mm for premature babies and used for airway management during surgical procedures and in PICU.

Now eight months old, we were fortunate that Leeds still had these smaller sized tubes for Cara's tiny airway because of their role as a teaching hospital. This tube was described as akin to a thin strand of spaghetti, being pumped continuously from a powerful ventilator which could snap at any time. Cara was third on the list for surgery that day with the fantastic Mr Crabbe (paediatric surgeon). There were two other cases, and all three were 'high emergency' cases.

The PICU doctor assured us that Mr Crabbe was one of the best and that he would be their choice if it were their child, which was reassuring. Cara was scheduled for theatre at 1pm that day, and it was then that we remembered her need for a christening.

Cara was blessed and baptised in intensive care by a priest who arrived 'straight from the golf course'. He was hyper, cracking jokes and mentioned how fortunate we were to find a priest on a Monday. This was usually their day of rest after a busy Sunday.

The nurses at the christening brought a gleaming white shawl which they placed on Cara during the blessing. After a quick sandwich and coffee, we returned to PICU before her 1pm transfer to the theatre.

We heard that the little boy with thick dark hair from the bed opposite was in trouble. The doctor's faces said it all. The little girl from Halifax was next up for surgery. This delay pushed Cara's operation back to 6pm.

We met with Mr Crabbe earlier that evening. The desolate October night reflected his mood. Something significant had happened earlier in surgery. After discussing the intricate procedure, he wished us well. Our friends from university in Liverpool arrived immediately afterwards.

Mike and Becky came to support us while Cara went to the theatre. It was a great source of comfort for us. The next time we saw Cara in PICU was with a Tracheostomy tube.

After spending time at her bedside, we went for coffee in the family room and met two sets of parents – one from the child facing Cara's station in PICU, and the other child from Halifax at Cara's right-hand side. We all hugged and bid each other well before driving home to rest, knowing that Cara was relatively safe and well with the Tracheostomy tube now in place.

Next morning, when back on the ward, we found that Cara tested positive for Respiratory Syncytial Virus (RSV) infection. RSV can cause a condition of the respiratory tract and lungs and endanger premature babies, infants, people with underlying health problems such as adults with heart and lung disease, the elderly, or people with compromised immune systems.

Cara began a two-week stint on PICU. The paediatric team introduced us to small tasks associated with Tracheostomy management such as suctioning secretions and cleaning the site around her throat.

Cara remained in the hospital for approximately two months until we were able to manage the Tracheostomy and deal with emergencies. The breathing tube may have been a lifesaver, but we were increasingly concerned about having to handle things in the real world.

Little Boy Passes Away

We visited a small Thai restaurant on Infirmary Street for a short break. Upon returning, we noticed the blue curtains enclosed around the young boy's bed facing Cara.

Entering the parent's room, we spotted the parents of the girl from Halifax. They were upset and explained how the boy had died during our lunch break. It happened five minutes before we left. It was turning into a miserable, sad day. It was painful to see the boy's parents collect his belongings and leave PICU with just his backpack by their side. We then realised that Cara was not out of the woods either.

Over the following week, as Cara battled RSV on the PICU ward, we met the lead nurse tasked with our training. Faye explained about her plans to return to work and how Copper Beech Nursery (linked to the Salvation Army - a charity that cares for the homeless and is involved in international disaster relief) had accepted Cara.

Initially, a member of the planning team warned us that it would be a struggle for the nursery to accept Cara because of the need for staff training and development. Feeling disheartened and panicked over her job, Faye returned home and called the nursery manager to explain the situation.

23

Rather than refuse, it was lovely to hear about their decision to train staff in Tracheostomy management. We shared contact numbers and arranged for Faye's return to work in March 2009, three months later.

A case meeting took place at the hospital involving various clinicians, nursery staff including Gemma and Gail, local council education representatives and the respite manager. Things were moving fast to prepare Cara for the outside world.

We then met with Julie White, a dedicated community nurse who discussed the process for transferring Cara back to home life. Julie was amazing and supported us in the early stages of Cara's life. We were sad to see her change role but proud when she became a Children's Oncology Macmillan Nurse Specialist. 11 years later, we bumped into Julie outside the children's oncology unit on our way to a meeting with Dr Sue Picton. What a twist of fate.

Part of the Tracheostomy training programme entailed pushing Cara through the back corridors of the hospital under the watchful eye of two healthcare professionals. Our tests took place one week apart. I went first, pushing the pram and equipment along the busy corridor. When the signal came, through the word 'Go' (meaning the breathing tube was blocked), it was time to stop immediately and act. Within seconds, Cara was hauled onto the cold vinyl floor.

An emergency Tracheostomy change was performed as the public, patients and clinicians strolled past. My gaze was fixed on the scissors, as the ties were cut. Holding the new device in my right hand, I gently removed the old tube - flinging it over my shoulder.

Using my left hand to avoid sudden head movements, I noticed how Cara looked confused before coughing. It was such a relief to insert the new tube and complete the intricate tie work to make sure it was safe and secure. The nurses then checked and confirmed that all was well. Faye performed a similar emergency exercise inside the hospital grounds before we could take her home.

Back Home

The doctors released Cara five days before Christmas. We were immediately confronted with life caring for a child with high-level medical needs. Our day trips to Bradford and Hebden Bridge were now off-limits. Over the next few months, we realised that the tube was a foreign body which gradually compromised her immune system.

Kelly, Amy, Gemma, Karen, Jermaine, and Mrs Jones from the Copper Beech Nursery successfully trained up to care for Cara which enabled Faye to return to work in March 2009. Over the next few years, our lives became medically orientated with countless sleepless nights due to Cara's frequent airway infections. It was tough going as I struggled to complete my PhD and Faye strived to hold down her job. Things were tight, and we just about managed to pay the bills each month.

Mr Crabbe then informed us that Cara needed significant tracheal surgery because the camera scope showed a compromised airway - the size of a premature baby (of approximately 29 weeks). It had never really grown - remaining tiny and in urgent need of intervention.

The first part of the procedure took place during summertime with fewer viruses around. One cold Sunday morning at home, I started to overthink the Tracheostomy tube change that was due to be completed that morning.

27

It was my turn, but for some reason, I wondered what would happen if the tube became stuck. Or if it did not enter as planned. The thought of losing Cara played on my mind, and by the time I started to prepare Cara for the change, it was as if she sensed my apprehension and reacted in kind.

Lifting her onto the changing table, she immediately started to fluster. Faye checked if I was OK just as Cara kicked her feet and started whimpering. My cold hands then touched her neck as the scissors cut through the tie holding the tube, and immediately she kicked off in convulsions – screaming and shaking.

Faye shouted at me to 'hurry up'. I pulled the old device out and noticed that the airway was bubbling with secretions as Cara went berserk. After a deep breath, I pushed the new tube into place as we sat her up and consoled her, before attempting to tie the knots.

It took several more attempts before I felt confident enough to perform another change. Gradually – we found a useful way to double-secure the knot, and things started to settle. Faye became the main Tracheostomy tube changer for a while as I took a step back, and we devised new ways to distract Cara while changing the tube.

For instance, having her sat upright on a little chair and singing was a good distraction. It was a running joke trying to find the old tube which we often flung over our shoulders in a panic.

After completing the care assessment and meeting the criteria of the Leeds Children's Nursing Dependency Score, a local respite centre for ill children in Leeds granted Cara up to four nights stay per month. Respite was a purpose-built unit for children with complex health needs. To us, it was a Godsend as the insomnia was wearing us down.

Our sleep would often be interrupted by the bubbling noise from Cara's Tracheostomy tube. After injecting some mils of saline (saltwater), the secretions required a suction machine, which sounded like a pneumatic drill to help clear her throat. Often afraid to sleep, we worried about the tube blocking overnight, which led to anticipatory unease and more sleepless nights. We just felt it was difficult to relax.

Over time, the lack of sleep and intense worry wore us down. Still, we were lucky to have family around or just a phone call away. The respite centre was a comforting place for sick children, equipped with creative playrooms, colourful wall designs and a circular multi-sensory room. It was also very much in-demand, with only a small number of bedrooms, a quiet place, and a bigger sitting room.

The open plan dining/activity area and an enclosed garden and patio area made it feel very homely and relaxing. Still, we were not naïve enough to think that it was normal for our family to be separated. We were often exhausted and desperate for a short break and time away together. Cara stayed with other children struggling with complex health needs, many of whom required a significant amount of nursing care.

She quickly acclimatised – but found the separation from us difficult to accept. After dropping off, Cara would wait and then wave from the bay window, often in tears.

We would also feel the same way, but the staff were brilliant, and she gradually started to enjoy her visits.

Cara met some friends including one little oxygen-confined girl in an electric wheelchair. She was giddy after hearing that Cara was coming to stay, and that made the trips to respite much more enjoyable.

The sweet sound of 'Hiiiiiii Cara' reverberated as soon we arrived. Staff often discussed their unique friendship, and how Cara loved dropping toys and paper on the floor for her friend to float around and collect them. They were like two peas in a pod.

On one occasion, after the cinema, Faye and I turned right at the bottom of the escalator and noticed Lisa, one of the staff members holding a child's hand.

As we crossed paths, our hearts sank as we realised that it was Cara. They were in front and did not see us.

My instinct was to shout over but knew that Cara would cry if she spotted us. We were fortunate to be living in Leeds Metropolitan Boundary rather than another postcode area.

For instance, we heard that Bradford had no overnight respite available for sick children at that time.

We developed a sound system for changing the tracheostomy tube until someone somewhere decided that Velcro straps should replace the ties securing the device. The new ties were supposed to be easier to administer and safer for Cara.

We tried the Velcro straps over two nights at our home and were concerned about the effect of sweat and how it loosened the stickiness of the ties. Cara sweated quite a bit due to her mop of curly hair and naturally, faffed about. We complained about the quality of the new ties after a near accident at home.

Shortly afterwards, Cara visited respite while Faye and I enjoyed our first break in weeks. Later that night, the phone rang: 'It's [respite]. Cara's absolutely fine, don't worry. But she was in the TV room watching a film (as we went to get Cara a drink). When we checked on her after a few minutes, she was sitting with the Tracheostomy tube in her hand, so we rushed her in for an emergency Tracheostomy change, and she's good as gold'. Our relief was palpable because Cara could not breathe for long without the tube, due to her narrow airway.

Surgery: Summer of 2009

A surprise phone call arrived during the summer of 2009, nine months after Cara's release from the hospital. It was Mr Crabbe's secretary, informing us about the date for surgery. It would involve a few weeks stay in hospital and some days in PICU.

We knew that part of Cara's rib would be removed and reattached to the lower airway in an intricate and quite perilous operation. The phone call arrived as we were on route to respite before catching a flight to Ireland to see family for two nights. It took the shine off our trip, and our fears about the pending surgery resurfaced.

The trip home to Belfast was quite emotional, and surgery proved to be the main topic of conversation. The quality family time benefited us greatly, and we returned to Leeds in good form, and optimistic that things might just be OK.

Faye took three weeks off from work for the operation. Colleagues frequently asked her, 'are you going anywhere nice on holiday', but she often joked 'The LGI'. Keeping Cara safe was our absolute priority.

Mr Crabbe met us on Sunday afternoon (before Monday's surgery) and reappeared for ward-round later that evening. He discussed everything, step-by-step before signing the dreaded yellow pre-operative form. After nothing by mouth ('nil par os'- NPO), Mr Crabbe scheduled a lunchtime operation which would last approximately six to seven hours.

Part of the procedure entailed converting segments from the rib cage and filing it into a hoop before reinserting into the lower airway. Cara would then return to PICU for some days. The plan was to keep her sedated until the airway swelling subsided and things remained in place.

On the morning of the operation, Cara desperately wanted food but could not speak. She kept pointing to the kitchen area, asking for milk in Makaton (sign language). We were choked but tried to keep her upbeat and occupied with frequent trips to the playroom.

It was then that the ward phone rang, and we got the go-ahead to walk Cara to the theatre. As we strolled down to the pre-theatre room, accompanied by nurses, emotions were running high as we approached the theatre door.

I then walked her through to the surgical team. As usual, they tried to keep things light-hearted, but Cara sensed the danger and panicked before the anaesthetic.

As we strolled outside in a daze, we began phoning our families to update them and asking for their prayers. The nurse took our mobile numbers before we left to attend lunchtime mass before walking aimlessly around town.

We were so beside ourselves that we cannot remember where we went or what we did after Mass until we headed back towards the hospital at around 6pm. As we passed the Chapel (Leeds Catholic Cathedral), we called in for another quick prayer.

It was empty apart from a nun who noticed Faye was carrying a picture of Padre Pio. She came over and touched Faye's hand. We discussed Cara's operation before the nun gently said 'she'll be OK, God's protecting her' before all three of us kneeled and prayed together.

On route to the hospital, the nurse called to say that the operation was almost finished. She then arranged for a post-operative meeting in the PICU parents' room. It was a mixture of relief and anxiety, wondering how it went and if she was OK. We sat for 10 minutes, where we met a kind Pakistani family from Bradford.

Their child had undergone major heart surgery just days previously. The clinicians could not detach him from the ventilator which affected his major organs. They then asked how we were doing and if it was our first time in PICU.

We explained that it was Cara's third time in intensive care (at that time) before the nurse popped her head around the corner to say that Cara was back from the theatre.

Upon entering the room full of beeping machines, we could see that Cara was heavily sedated and intubated. A fresh-faced Mr Crabbe then appeared, grinning widely, in regular attire, out of his blue scrubs.

He explained how the operation had gone well. The plan was to let her rest by staying sedated for a few days and 'we'd take it from there'. Overjoyed and relieved, we headed home to Bramley for some rest.

After two nights of intensive care, the clinicians were relatively happy with Cara, and her saturation levels had improved. They quickly arranged a transfer to the children's ward. The plan was to slowly wean her off the morphine, which proved to be a tough ask. We then noticed the little boys' parents who were sitting in the next bed, talking to the Consultant.

We could sense by the tone of the conversation that things were pear-shaped. There was mention of failing kidneys and sadly, little likelihood of survival because of other complications. His parents then called their family to explain how dialysis was their last hope, but it was not looking good. Just then, a blue screen was pulled around his bed, as the call came for Cara to be moved.

We asked one of the PICU nurses afterwards if he had made it. She could not say for confidentiality reasons, but we could tell it was unlikely, judging by her body language and depth of sadness in her face.

Cara was prepared for release after four days of sedatives on the children's ward. It was a relief to return home after things had gone so well. Respite staff called to discuss the operation. They offered Cara two extra nights for the following week, so we visited our friend John Croke in London.

Just before leaving, Cara bum-shuffled in her nappy in front of her grandparents David and Hazel. She then rested her hands on the ground and rocked before crawling for the first time. A beautiful moment that we'll always cherish.

John's Godchild was ill in hospital after surgery around that time. We crammed everything possible into the two-day trip before returning to collect Cara from respite.

Approximately six months later, a bronchoscopy was performed to assess her lungs and airway. The segment of rib had deviated from its initial position but fortunately wasn't a significant problem.

We continued doing Tracheostomy changes and made frequent trips to respite.

Still, we were curious as to when the tube could be removed and bugged Mr Crabbe's secretary with regular phone calls about the next step.

Faye and I eventually visited Mr Crabbe, who informed us that Cara would require the Tracheostomy for substantially longer than expected (years, not months).

We were hoping that decannulation would occur shortly after the rib surgery.

He also explained the significant risks involved and preferred to wait and see if Cara's airway would develop naturally and thus potentially avoid further surgery.

What a shock! Tracheostomy management and respite would continue for a while yet. It was time for Cara's first trip to Ireland.

First Trip to Ireland

Cara was three years old when she first visited her family in Belfast. It was late September, and we wanted to travel before the weather changed. Susceptible to winter bugs, Cara was frequently unwell due to bacterial and viral infections, including pneumonia.

We packed up the medical equipment, including the nebuliser (vaporiser), suction machine, Tracheostomy tubes and protective bibs. Cara had packed her bag well in advance, and she was excited to bring some new dresses.

Off we went from Leeds Bradford airport on an 11am flight. We stayed at a nice hotel in Belfast for a treat because it was Cara's first trip abroad.

Our family waited in anticipation of Cara's arrival. She was proud to wear a new dress as we headed up the Falls Road for the family party. As we pulled into my mum's street, Cara's face lit when she spotted the house was decked in balloons and signs saying: 'Welcome Home Cara'.

My sister Donna and Cara met for the first time, so it was a particularly memorable trip. The look in Cara's eyes told us that we could never visit Ireland again without her.

My sister Sarah bought Cara a fluffy rabbit from the 'Build-a-Bear' workshop. Afterwards, she went to Sarah's house with her cousins Jack and Ciara for ice cream.

That Sunday, after a nebuliser, we went to a local restaurant on the Andersonstown (Andytown) Road for dinner. She loved the live Irish traditional music, and it was brilliant to see her run and dance so care-free with her cousins. It was important to keep our wits about us and frequently check Cara's Tracheostomy tube while she played. But the suction machine was close by together with a handy back-up kit for emergencies. So, the trip was a tricky one to plan and manage. But looking back, we enjoyed precious family time.

Trial Ward Decannulation

As Cara approached her fourth birthday, we received a call from Mr Crabbe's secretary to explain the plan for a trial decannulation. Removing the tube would enable Cara to breathe, unassisted.

We visited the children's ward that Monday morning. Cara was given a ward bed in preparation for the procedure. Mr Crabbe arrived around dinner time and sat next to Cara on the bed. He gently undid the ties while casually talking and slowly removed the Tracheostomy tube.

We expected this to happen in the theatre. The act of removing it manually in the busy ward caught us by surprise. After attaching her finger to the saturation machine, he explained how she would be monitored and observed over the coming days. We were delighted to observe Cara without the tube but found it difficult to digest the enormity of what had just happened.

We learnt from experience to take turns sleeping overnight on the ward. Two tired minds and exhausted bodies were of little use to Cara during the day when she was at her most active. We often experienced insomnia on the lively children's wards.

Cara also struggled to sleep. A concoction of beeping saturation machines; computer games; mobile phones; and blaring televisions while sick children and infants frequently cried through the night.

Now it was my turn to stay overnight. Laying alongside Cara, I counted breaths and recognised a change in her breathing pattern. She was uncomfortable and shifted positions before dozing off. Between gasps, I was mindful that the saturation machine showed fluctuating oxygen levels. She was sometimes dropping to high 70s before shooting back to the low 90s, hovering and then falling to the 80s before finally, drifting higher to +95%. Like an aeroplane, dropping down in a storm before shooting back up amongst the clouds to safety. I would close my eyes and pray for Cara, for our family who were all deeply concerned, and for a short bout of uninterrupted sleep.

Four straight hours of sleep is all we ever wished for on the wards. Any semblance of a decent sleep felt like a small and vital win and helped us to cope better. Less than four hours of sleep felt like mental torture, and the unease kicked in. We would often be jolted from our sleep and immediately check if Cara was breathing correctly; the colour of her lips; and numbers on the saturation machine.

We often quizzed the nurses when they arrived to reposition her. They would either wait and observe or provide a whiff of oxygen under her nose which often did the trick. Once her oxygen levels rose towards 100%, we would drift off again, dozing while listening to our iPod, before frequently awakening to the noise of her breathing. It felt like a cat and mouse game.

Next morning, after some broken sleep, I took a quick shower then grabbed toast and tea from the kitchen. When I returned, Cara was sitting up, eating a bowl of cereal but looking tired and sad. We found this odd, because she often looked OK, even when unwell.

Faye soon arrived in time for the ward round. We then spoke to Mr Crabbe and his team. They checked Cara and decided to play it by ear for another night because she was starting to maintain her oxygen levels.

On the second day without the Tracheostomy tube, we drove to the Abbey Inn on Pollard Road for a coffee. This traditional pub is situated next to the Leeds Liverpool Canal. It is supposed to be a haunted space (due to previously being a mortuary until the late 1950s). Morgue staff laid bodies on slabs at the site of the current pool table (5). The building itself feels a bit spooky, but it's a quirky bar on a lovely setting next to the Leeds and Liverpool Canal. We would often walk from Bramley to the leafy area by the canal and then up the hill to Horsforth, which had some great places to eat and drink.

We sat outside and observed Cara before driving onto a Chinese restaurant on Vicar Lane. We watched her like a hawk and don't remember much about the food. It was fascinating but frightening, because we were terrified of her choking or collapsing. She looked pale and grew increasingly quieter as the day went on, so we returned to the ward for an assessment.

I swapped with Faye and travelled home for some rest but couldn't stop thinking about Cara and the next step. Faye called early the next morning with news that I didn't want to hear. Evidently, the second night was much worse. The saturation machine was frequently beeping, but the nurses described it as a relatively normal response as her body readjusts. There was even the possibility of being released home the following day. But Faye thought otherwise and had a gut feeling that things were heading South.

After the nurses changed shifts, Faye discussed events with the ward sister and requested a chat with Mr Crabbe. After some breakfast, she returned to find Mr Crabbe by Cara's bedside, checking her over.

Faye remarked that Cara was not ready for home, and Mr Crabbe agreed. Cara's stridor meant that the Tracheostomy days were back.

After checking the open airway, he noticed that it had already started to close and decided to take Cara back to the theatre to reopen the airway for cannulation.

Feeling despondent, we asked ourselves if it was good luck or bad luck? The potential for some relative normality in our home lives had disappeared after two eventful days.

Simultaneously, there was contentment because the tube was also a lifesaver. Faye cried; and as Mr Crabbe walked off, the ward nurse arrived and comforted her.

She then called and explained the news to me, and I remember feeling devastated, but knew deep down that it was not the right time.

Later that evening, after cannulation, Mr Crabbe called by and explained that after checking things over in theatre, he noticed some floppiness in the upper part of the airway.

Cara required more risky surgery to correct this problem using cartilage from the other rib cage.

Mr Crabbe planned to operate in October 2012, and she would soon have prominent scars under each part of her chest alongside the deep scar on her throat.

The following morning, we made an emotional trip back home with Cara. We then discussed plans to attend a family wedding and wondered if it was possible to bring Cara on her first trip to Spain. Carole Appleby, the outreach community nurse, confirmed that we could travel with medical insurance, a medical waiver and medical equipment. Carole became reacquainted with Cara years later as a Macmillan nurse (after the brainstem tumour diagnosis).

Tanzanian Irish Wedding

We received an invite to the wedding of my sister Lisa and her Tanzanian husband Albert and decided to travel just six weeks before the wedding at the Cala D'or Yacht Club in Majorca.

Faye called Sarah, who was working at the Royal Victoria Hospital in Belfast to share the good news. She was delighted to hear that Cara would be an extra bridesmaid.

The whole family was buzzing with excitement. This would be our first trip abroad (beyond Ireland) with Cara and our first trip to Spain for almost five years. After arranging the medical insurance, we bought Cara an ivory bridesmaid's dress at Monsoon.

A medical note from Dr Phil Chetcuti confirmed that she was fit to fly. Next up was the hospital equipment pool which provided us with an extra medical kit including a lighter travel nebuliser.

The night before flying was hectic, especially after receiving the news that Georgina and Rocco (our friends) were expecting their first child. After waking and dressing Cara, we gave her a steam nebuliser before heading to Leeds Bradford Airport.

As we entered the airport lounge, we noticed that a new restaurant had just opened. We tucked into healthy fish and eggs (on the house) while Cara was true to form with her mini fry. The flights and transfers were swift. But she was in desperate need of a nebuliser to moisten the airway upon arrival at the hotel. We used lots of saline to prevent the tube from blocking.

Still, the thick secretions meant trouble and Cara needed a proper nebuliser urgently. After preparing the device, we were surprised to find a problem with the power source.

Maintenance staff quickly sorted the problem, and her breathing improved after 20 minutes of steam. Cara proudly got dressed into her first swimming costume, and off we went to the local café directly facing our hotel for lunch.

The location was perfect. It was next to the Cala Gran beach and within walking distance to the main restaurant areas. We were exhausted but celebrated Cara's first trip to Majorca with a drink. Still, we remained vigilant because of the dangers associated with the Tracheostomy tube.

After getting sorted on the beach, it was time to enter the picturesque coves. The look on Cara's face as she paddled in the sea for the first time was unforgettable and priceless.

She wore a Swedish Nose cap that filtered the air and a Tracheostomy bib with extra tape. These medical items provided extra layers of protection and kept the sand and water out. Four days of quiet family time was ideal before what seemed like half of Belfast arrived for the wedding.

My brother Damien and his wife Jacqui booked into the hotel opposite ours. The rest of my family stayed in Cala Millor. Two days before the wedding, Lisa and Albert made final arrangements at the Yacht Club.

We met with family afterwards at our local café before everyone headed to the beach. On the day of Lisa's wedding, we advised the wedding party to watch over Cara and her cousins.

There were small pools dotted around the venue, and we were conscious that the immersion of her Tracheostomy tube in water could prove deadly. But the wedding day was perfect.

It was a great get-together after so many years being apart. Close family and friends travelled, including Gerard and Joanne and their family.

Next day, we were sad to leave and return to Leeds. We managed to grab some lunch with Lisa and Albert before the flight. Cara went on a final shopping trip with Damien and Jacqui. She returned dressed like a senorita with a red traditional Spanish dress and black dance shoes.

Magoo looked gorgeous but walked like she drank the bar dry in her Spanish heels. It was a great end to a beautiful wedding and holiday.

Surgery After starting School

Before Cala D'or, a plan was developed for Cara's schooling and to manage the transition from nursery to Bramley St Peter's Primary School. Surgery was due in November 2012, a few months afterwards.

Clinicians put a care plan in place to manage the Tracheostomy. Faye accompanied Cara to the school each Tuesday afternoon which helped her to settle in.

Faye was Tracheostomy trained in case of an emergency and would often sit in the reception area. Cara's teacher Miss Thomas knew that she was close by if needed. She passed her time reading books such as Patti Smith's 'Just Kids'.

I took Faye to a few Patti Smith concerts in Leeds and Scarborough. On one occasion, Faye spoke to Patti and mentioned that I took her there for a birthday treat.

Patti then gathered her bandmates and some fans in a circle and serenaded Faye with 'Happy Birthday'. Everyone cheered as Patti boarded the tour bus. What a great night!

Latrice, the nursery support worker would accompany Cara to the school on Wednesday through to Friday afternoons which enabled our return to work. Cara's team decided against further staff training because of the length of time (two months) needed to be Tracheostomy competent.

Mr Crabbe planned for surgery shortly afterwards. Cara settled well at school, and November came around before we knew it. Here we were, back at square one, in the LGI on a Sunday evening to prepare for Monday's surgery. It was a strange experience walking through the German Christmas Market in Millennium Square.

Before entering the hospital, we stopped to buy sweets and took a lovely picture of Cara in her bright red coat with massive curls. Still, it was tough trying to smile, knowing that another life-threatening operation was pending.

After getting unpacked at the bedside, Mr Crabbe arrived for a pre-operative chat on Sunday evening. Later that night, we both decided to stay over.

The anaesthetist who had previously worked with Cara took medical observations. Something was causing her heart rate to become slightly raised, and thick secretions led to a rattle noise.

By midnight, the physio arrived and performed chest exercises. At the same time, they administered extra nebulisers to clear the secretions.

The anaesthetist was '50/50' whether surgery should proceed but agreed to check the next morning and discuss with Mr Crabbe.

Right enough, Cara was deemed to be fit for surgery after an early meeting with the clinical team and placed first on the list for the 8.30am procedure.

We were both exhausted and concerned but freshened up with showers and breakfast in preparation for the long day ahead.

51

At 8.30am sharp, the short and emotional walk to the theatre began. The nurse tried to ease Cara's concerns by discussing clothes and jewellery. But Cara was overwhelmed and lost in her thoughts. After entering the pre-surgery room, she became distressed and panicky.

The team tried to ease the tension with light-hearted stories and jokes which did not go down so well. Cara looked at me, wondering why I wasn't protecting her and asking why I was putting her through surgery again.

It was tough watching as she fought against the gas effects before drifting off. The team and I lifted her onto the bed. I will never forget the pungent gas fumes coupled with her dead-weight as she flopped in my arms.

Faye and I then made the long stroll out of the hospital and across to the early morning mass at the local chapel where we sat quietly at the back and lit two candles. We remember watching the flames flickering madly as we left to do another random and forgetful walk around Leeds.

But this time, unlike the previous operation during summertime, it was frosty and dreary, which added to the sense of fear and apprehension.

Six hours later, we headed back to the hospital, where the nurse directed us to the intensive care unit. The ward sister told us that Cara was in recovery. Mr Crabbe and the team would bring her in a sedated state. She would remain that way until swelling from the reconstructive work subsided. The surgery which entailed using rib-cartilage for the upper airway went relatively well so we drove home for a rest.

Next day, we returned and noticed that somebody had moved Cara to a side room because the sputum sample showed another RSV infection. Cara was still sedated at this stage and would remain like that until Thursday, four days later.

Mr Crabbe then told us to arrive in intensive care by 8.30am on Thursday when they would start to ease her off the sedation medication

When we entered on Thursday morning, Cara was already half sat up and appeared frantic as the nurse tried to console her. The staff were ready to return to the theatre and remove her from the ventilator.

Shortly afterwards, the ward nurse received a call that Cara was now returning to PICU.

We immediately noticed that the Tracheostomy tube was gone. She was tugging around the neck and had a weak voice, so the nurse checked her saturation levels, and oxygen was immediately provided.

Again, we were both elated but noticed how she gradually required more oxygen and was struggling to breathe.

The medical team then paged Mr Crabbe. After some discussions, the team told us that any further deterioration would mean returning to theatre for the tube to be cannulated (reinserted).

We made family calls before we returned to the side unit where we noticed that Cara was now on C-PAP (continuous positive airway pressure).

This intervention was a type of positive airway pressure ventilator being used to apply mild air pressure, continually, while she recovered. It was uncomfortable but proved effective for keeping a continuous airflow. C-PAP supported more spontaneous breathing, enabling Cara to breathe on her own while keeping her airway unobstructed. We sat with Cara over the next few hours, anticipating a return to the theatre.

Surprisingly, the medical team were happy with the saturation levels and felt no need to reinsert the Tracheostomy tube. Happy days! It seemed like we had just won the lottery but were conscious that things could change.

When Cara drifted off to sleep at around 8pm, we were advised to return home to rest. Next morning, we returned to the intensive care unit and saw that Cara was sitting upright with an oxygen tube under her nose. The nurse explained that Cara would use the C-PAP as-and-when needed and would alternate with an oxygen tube.

When Cara spoke, her voice was audibly hushed – almost a whisper. The nurse advised that it might be due to swelling, but to prepare for the possibility that her vocal cords may have been damaged in surgery.

When Faye cuddled Cara, she whispered 'go and buy me a microphone' ??. Again, we all needed that laugh, and after a few hours, she faded with tiredness. The nurse again used C-PAP to support her breathing while she slept. After lunch, we bought a toy plastic microphone to keep her entertained.

The Consultants explained later that Cara would need one week of close observation before a decision is made to transfer her onto the children's ward.

The recuperation process would delay Cara's return to school until after the new year. Faye took more time off work on unpaid leave, and my studies took a back seat once again as we sat things out at the hospital with Cara. Luckily, I was well supported by Dr David Allen, the AIMTech Research Group and Leeds University Business School during these tough early years with Cara. I managed to find time to work off-line on my PhD in the hospital canteen and by Cara's bedside. My laptop was out wherever the opportunity arose, which also helped to take my mind off things.

Little Girl from Bradford

Over the next week on intensive care, Cara had ups and downs and often needed C-PAP. They brought in a mobile television and DVD player.

Cara's choice of film was 'High School Musical' (6). The movie was played repeatedly from morning until night for several days. Cara loved it so we couldn't argue.

As the week went on, an Asian family from Bradford met us in the parent's room. They told us about their little girl's condition. There were few words, but they looked overwhelmed, and we could tell that it was dire.

That Sunday, the Consultant felt that Cara was well enough to go onto the ward for a shower because she was coping better without oxygen and just needed C-PAP in the evening.

We took her down in a wheelchair and got her washed and changed before returning to her intensive care bed.

Faye's folks were unable to visit the intensive care unit because of a global flu pandemic at that time.

As we left the elevator, the little girl's sizable family sat outside, looking stressed and strained.

We knew something wasn't right, and after ringing to enter, the intensive care nurse allowed us through.

Walking towards Cara's side room off reception, we noticed that the blue screen had surrounded the little girl's bed directly opposite. Just earlier that day, we left a box of chocolates for the staff.

When we walked by with Cara, we noticed two doctors eating while engaged in a quiet conversation.

Moments later, they walked at a snail's pace towards the blue screen. Faye remarked to the nurse that things didn't look right. She sadly nodded in agreement.

Just then, both doctors followed the parents into a private side room. We knew from Cara's experience in intensive care that things were deteriorating.

A stream of family members strolled past on their way to seeing the child. The child's nurse (senior sister) joined us to give the family some space.

Quite a few other doctors then visited Cara. We could tell from their expressions that they were leaving the family to say their goodbyes. The last beeps from the saturation monitor were audible before it flatlined.

The sound of wailing soon replaced an eerie silence. Faye broke down too. We found it difficult to comprehend another death of a child so soon after the previous loss.

The senior sister then confirmed that the child had passed away. We explained that this was the third death that we had experienced in intensive care. Still, she found that surprising, saying that it was very unusual. Perhaps she was trying to alleviate our fears. After preparing Cara for bed, we visited the family and paid our respects in the parent's room. They warmly greeted us and appreciated the gesture but were devastated. I remember pulling the car over for a few minutes on the way home because Faye felt so ill. Another crazy sad day and another family in mourning.

That Monday, we spoke to Mr Crabbe, who was happy with Cara's progress even though she was still tugging around her neck. The team transferred Cara onto the ward, where we stayed for another week – taking turns to sleep overnight. Faye's folks were soon able to visit which took the pressure off us until her release.

We were so glad to get Cara home, but she still struggled. After three days at home, we let her sleep in the afternoon, but her shoulders began rising, ribs sucking in, and she seemed increasingly agitated. We drove her down to A&E, where somebody admitted her onto the ward.

That night, Faye stayed over with Cara as I returned home, with flu symptoms. I bought some hot and sour soup from the Chinese restaurant, packed full of hot green chillies before resting. Next morning, it was gutting to hear that Cara had struggled overnight, needing oxygen. The doctors requested a bed on the respiratory unit to perform a sleep test. I travelled down to the hospital and feeling increasingly unwell, was unable to swap with Faye.

Instead, we called Cara's Grandad David, who decided to sleep overnight at the hospital with Cara. Faye stayed with Cara until later that evening before the doctor transferred her to the respiratory ward. An x-ray showed that she had a chest infection. The doctor decided to reschedule the sleep test for a few days. This delay would provide space for the 'intravenous antibiotics' to do their magic.

Over the next four days, Faye and her dad took turns to sleep over, and Hazel (Faye's mum) cared for Cara during the day. During Cara's evening meal, Faye cleared her head by walking through town in Leeds. She remembers feeling lost because of the build-up to Christmas and the sights and sounds of families enjoying themselves. At the same time, the magical Christmas feeling seemed to be missing for us.

Cara improved dramatically that Thursday night and was now ready for the sleep test. The nurse attached the device to her ear, and thankfully, she managed to sleep through the night. The sleep-test data was collated and fed through the hospital information system to Cara's care records. Next morning, Dr Phil Chetcuti was at the nursing station. Faye asked: 'what are you doing here', to which Phil replied in his sarcastic voice, 'Well I do work here, Faye'. Phil was always the joker and a great guy.

He would always listen to us as parents and put everyone at ease. We were glad to be involved in the conversations and big decisions, and Phil took a whole patient and family-centred approach, which we deeply appreciated. Faye's dad then arrived as Phil strolled in and explained the excellent sleep test results to Faye before subsequently discharging Cara.

By then, I was feeling much better, so I drove down to collect Faye and Cara from the back of the hospital, at the Clarendon Wing. Christmas was fast approaching, with five days to go, and we were so glad and relieved to get her home. There was no trip planned to see family in Belfast that year because Cara was unable to fly. Still, it was our first Christmas without the Tracheostomy tube, so it felt perfect. On my birthday on New Year's Eve, Faye surprised me with a meal in York at Café Rouge. This trip was our first without the large, noisy suction machine and Tracheostomy management kit. It was strange to see Cara breathing unaided, and she was coping well.

York is a medieval city and felt very Christmassy. After the meal, we went for a quick drink at a cellar bar before travelling home. Within no time, Cara was in her pyjamas and out for the count, as we sat up past midnight and enjoyed a quiet but special time reflecting on the past year.

In the new year, Faye returned to work, and Cara returned to school full time. Three months later, Cara had a scope performed by Mr Crabbe to check for scarring. He explained that the noisy breathing overnight was normal and that we should expect to see things settle.

Cara's health improved over the next six months, so that summer we flew to Spain for a family holiday. The first week was fantastic, but the second turned into a nightmare because we had no idea that chlorine from the pool and air conditioning could lead to airway problems.

It was at this point that we realised that she was suffering from intermittent bouts of sleep apnoea. It became a game of cat and mouse as the normality that we craved wasn't happening. The frequency of hospital appointments over the next few years meant that the hospital doctors never managed to sign Cara off from the hospital.

Cara's Breathing Exercises

Cara was happy in her own little world and tended to blank out problems. She was a daydreamer and struggled to concentrate on specific tasks that we had set for her. We encouraged breathing exercises such as Buteyko Method (7) devised by Prof. Konstantin Buteyko, or 4-7-8 breathing technique by Dr Weil, the founder and director of the University of Arizona Centre for Integrative Medicine.

The 4-7-8 breathing technique required Cara to take long, deep breaths through the nose for four seconds, holding for seven seconds, and out for eight through the mouth (to be performed ten times in a row). We realised that rhythmic breathing promoted relaxation, reduced feelings of anxiety and controlled and reduced Cara's tendency to rebel against doing the exercises, which was understandable. Harvard Health Publishing reports that:

> *Deep breathing also goes by the names of Diaphragmatic Breathing, Abdominal Breathing, Belly Breathing, and Paced Respiration. By breathing deeply, the air coming in through the nose fully fills the lungs, and the lower belly rises. For many of us, deep breathing seems unnatural...*
> *There are several reasons for this. For one, a poor body image is negatively related to respiration in western culture. A flat stomach is considered attractive, and people may often hold in their stomach muscles. This interferes with deep breathing and gradually makes shallow "Chest Breathing" seem reasonable, which increases tension and anxiety.*

Shallow breathing limits the diaphragm's range of motion. The lowest part of the lungs doesn't get a full share of oxygenated air. That can make you feel short of breath and anxious.

Deep abdominal breathing encourages full oxygen exchange — That is, the beneficial trade of incoming oxygen for outgoing Carbon Dioxide. Not surprisingly, it can slow the heartbeat and lower or stabilise blood pressure (8).

Our friend, Terry Boyle (RIP, September 2020) often confirmed the positive effects of 4-7-8 breathing by testing it using a personal blood pressure machine. Cara enjoyed her small mindfulness class in Horsforth, Leeds and loved yoga. She had immense upper body strength, taking great pleasure in practising martial arts techniques on me when I wasn't expecting it.

Cara was resilient and courageous, but also very sensitive, introverted and emotionally intelligent. But her lungs were compromised, so we continued to alternate 4-7-8 breathing with Buteyko breathing, to develop healthier breathing patterns and more regular oxygen-to-carbon-dioxide ratios in her bloodstream.

We read how people with breathing problems, including asthmatics, had benefited greatly through these techniques, which enhanced feelings of wellbeing and reduced dependency on medication.

In the late-19th century, Austrian scientists Breyer & Gering discovered that man is the only biological specimen on Earth not to have developed a correct way of breathing – some of us breathe deeply, others superficially, some fast, some slow, some with pauses, some without.

Prof. Buteyko's later research showed that only around one in ten of us breathe correctly, giving a very specific gas mixture which, our organism requires to function correctly. So how should we breathe?

Physiological norms apply to pulse, blood pressure, sugar levels, temperature – and breathing. At rest, an adult should ideally breathe lightly, superficially and through the nose. A healthy person can perform light exercise and still breathe lightly, while a sick person needs deep breaths almost constantly (9).

First New Years in Belfast

After discussing the potential of adoption with Cara at Horsforth Park, we attended preliminary adoption meetings before an adoption team visited us at our home. The woman in charge advised that we had already gone through a significant and traumatic time in recent years and to take six months out as a family before returning and continuing with the application.

Over time, we discussed how special it would be for Cara to have her own little brother or sister. This time to reflect proved to be precious. Curious why Cara was born so early, we visited a hospital specialist to discuss the premature birth and were delighted to hear that the chances of the same thing happening were slim. They arranged for Faye to be closely monitored if-and-when she did fall pregnant. The doctors attributed Cara's early birth to a bleed in the womb, and this tiny bleed was apparently enough to instigate early labour

Soon afterwards, we took our first 'New Years Eve' trip to Ireland with Cara for joint birthday celebrations. The atmosphere was electric, as family and friends gathered at my mothers' house. We come from prominent families anyway, with 11 siblings in my father's side and 13 on my mother's side, with my mum, the eldest and John the youngest. Cara met up again with her aunts, uncles and cousins including the Lwakatare (Tanzanian-Irish) clan; Jacqui and Jack, and the Kelly's including Jack 'the footballer' and Chloe; and her big cousins Sean, Ciara and Kirsty.

This was precisely how we imagined Cara to react. Coming from a small family in Leeds and unable to travel for health reasons, Cara was now confronted with the love and pandemonium of her big Irish family.

Cara was delighted with all the hugs, presents and treats. We arrived on the 30th December to celebrate Kirsty's 21st birthday at a pizza restaurant in Andytown.

As usual, we visited my mum's house for one-for-the-road before heading back to our hotel in Belfast city centre. Next day, Faye and Cara treated me at Zen's Chinese restaurant for a birthday lunch, before the full birthday celebrations kicked off.

My mum and I share birthday dates (31.12.74 v. 31.12.47), so there is always an extra excuse to celebrate. We then spent some family time at another restaurant before returning to my mum's house for the New Year's festivities. On a previous New Years trip to Ireland, Faye and I went to meet Sarah's husband Gerry's folks, Joan, and Gerry Senior.

A house party was in full flow as we knocked on the door before being invited in by a slightly familiar face.

It soon dawned that we did not know anyone in the house before quickly departing. We had entered the wrong house but eventually made it to Joan's, and Gerry Senior had prepared his usual 'whiskey special'. Faye often jokes how I left their house every New Year's Eve looking like 'Reddy Rooster' after the hefty tipple.

Big Sister Cara

From January 2014, we began to try for another child. During a holiday in Majorca in August that year with my mum and Aunt Barbara, I remember how we all sat on the beach as my mum hugged and sang to Cara. She was fascinated by Christy Moore's lyrics (or Christy Murray Mint) as she endearingly called him. Being a little dreamer herself, she loved 'Reel in the Flickering Light' (10).

As I Was Walking Home One Evenin'
I Know This Takes Some Believin'
I Met a Group of Creatures
With the Strangest Lookin' Features
A Poor Old Dove and a Worm in the Weed
And a Fine Old Pigeon, Yes Indeed
A Daddy Longlegs Jumped Up Sprightly
As He Danced to the Reel in the Flickering Light...

On His Thin and Wispy Spindles
He Was Deft and He Was Nimble
His Eyes Were Scientific
And His Dancing Was Terrific
And the Rats and Worms They Made a Din
And the Nettles in the Corners Took It in
"Oh God" Says I, "Tonight's the Night"
"We'll Dance to the Reel in the Flickering Light"
Oh Round We Go, Heel to the Toe
"Oh God" Says I "Tonight's the Night

Looking back, we can see where Cara got her imagination from. After returning from Majorca, Faye felt nauseous and undertook a pregnancy test at home shortly before her birthday. The result was positive, and we were absolutely buzzing at the news. But after Cara's troubles, we were conscious about the prospect of another early labour. Cara was delighted to have a sibling on the way and brought her little teddy bears to our bed to celebrate.

Faye called the doctor to arrange an appointment with the midwife. Shortly afterwards, the hospital assigned a clinical specialist because of the previous complications. Faye's scan was on Christmas Eve morning with Mr Simpson, and Cara accompanied us to the hospital. We introduced Cara to Mr Simpson, and he was chuffed to receive a cake that she had baked for him earlier that morning. Pointing to the baby on the screen, he asked if it was going to be 'pink or blue', but we decided not to know. So long as the child was healthy. Cara was delighted to see the heartbeat on the screen. She was glad to see the scan pictures with some additional images provided for Cara.

Later, Faye went for another scan some weeks before birth, and as suspected, it was a breech. We declined the offer to physically turn the baby. We were then given a C-Section date for 30th April, one week before the original due date. The doctor discussed the risks before we signed the yellow pre-operative form. Cara seemed to recognise the form from her own experiences of surgery, and like role-reversal, tapped Faye gently on the shoulder to reassure her. The build-up to the birth had now started in earnest, and we were all eagerly anticipating the new arrival.

Cara stayed with her grandparents on the night before Finn's birth. We arrived at the hospital for 7am and were taken straight to the pre-operative room.

It was strange entering this controlled environment compared to Cara's early arrival. Faye had an initial scan to see if the child was still breeched before the doctors proceeded with an epidural injection into her lower back.

The anaesthetist took almost one hour to get the needle into the correct position before Faye's transfer to the theatre.

It was a bright but chilly room, with several clinicians and the midwife laughing and joking while the radio played music in the background. We did not know the child's gender beforehand and preferred the element of surprise.

The Midwife told Faye to expect the feeling of 'someone doing the washing-up' in her stomach. And that is exactly how she described it afterwards, down to a tee.

Within minutes, the Midwife lifted the baby from Faye who struggled to see past the top of his head. One of them pointed to Finn's widget and asked, 'what's that?', to which I replied, 'a baby'.

Then they said, no, what sex is it? That's when I shouted, 'Is it a wee boy'. The Midwife then said, 'of course it's a boy'.

I previously confused the umbilical cord during Cara's birth and wasn't prepared to make the same mistake.

She then placed Finn on Faye's skin, and we were both on cloud nine, and just so excited to tell Cara that she now had a little brother (Mr McGinty as we call him) and was finally a big sister.

Things quickly went pear-shaped amidst the excitement. The midwife was concerned that Finn was struggling to breathe. The paediatrician arrived and after initial checks, prescribed antibiotics as back up because of Faye's Strep B diagnosis before birth.

Simultaneously, Faye's vision went, and she reported a buzzing sound in her ears. The Midwife informed the anaesthetist before she strayed into hypothermia which included shivers, pale skin, breathlessness, rapid breathing, and exhaustion.

The anaesthetist recognised how confused Faye had become and kept asking 'where are you' and 'can you tell me where you are'?'

My role was to stay calm and to keep Faye alert by reassuring her. After some hysterical shouting and panic, her body temperature hovered at 21 degrees, before they managed to work their magic.

The clinical team worked quickly and effectively to get her back towards 35 degrees Celsius. When an adult's temperature drops to 32C or below, the shivering may cease as blackout beckons, which is treacherous.

Thankfully, she improved and was comforted with extra warm blankets and heating pads. She continued to stabilise in the High Dependency Unit. I remembered that Faye had not eaten from 7pm the night before and decided to buy her a fresh pizza slice from the hospital canteen.

After her first bite, the midwife appeared and told me off for buying junk food after a critical incident. Pizza was one of the worst things to eat after a C-Section. The fresh dough expands in the stomach and certainly was not sensible after Faye's stomach had been stapled.

Faye gradually recovered from the hypothermia as her folks, sister Lucy and Cara appeared by the hospital bedside. Cara got to meet Finn for the first time and was immediately smitten.

Faye bought Cara two little Disney toys from Frozen, as a present from Finn. Over the next few months, we adapted to having a new-born again after a seven-year break.

The strangest feeling was bringing Finn straight home from hospital compared to our experience with Cara on neonatal and waiting for months to get home.

The house went from relative calm to chaos, as Cara and Finn bonded and got up to all sorts of mischief. We would often hear Cara talking to Finn in his Moses basket and checking that he was OK.

Cara almost finished her summer school term, so we booked a trip to Salou in Spain because of its cooler climate compared to the Canary Islands (our usual destinations) and a quick two-hour flight and transfer. Off we went with Finn's buggy and suitcases to the airport. Cara had her unique bag which she had spent weeks packing. Always so organised when it came to travel. Everything was in place, neat and tidy.

The trip itself was fine, but once again, chlorine from the pool had a profound effect on Cara's airway and took the shine off the end of the holiday.

We grew gradually worried for Cara while trying to manage Finn, who was just four months old. We were glad to return home but realised that these airway problems were still capable of causing significant problems. Faye then returned to work at the University.

It was then that we decided to move to a new house, in a better area for the kids. We always liked the Horsforth area, and its proximity to the airport and city centre, and decided to move in that direction. 'Donegal Pauline' as we knew her, and her family run a pub in Horsforth. Cara became a regular visitor, especially when we watched the live soccer, Gaelic football and hurling matches.

Christening Before House Move

Cara and Finn were both christened together in September 2015. Our friends Dee and Bridgeen stood for Finn (became Finn's Godparents). This time, Cara managed to have a proper Irish Christening with a party afterwards. Some years earlier, I was chuffed to be Godfather for Dee's son, John.

It was lovely to get a joint blessing for the kids at St Paul's Chapel on the Falls Road in Belfast. The celebrations continued afterwards at the Glenowen restaurant. Damien and Jacqui previously stood for Cara (in theory – on paper) because her christening occurred in intensive care in Leeds. But this time, the whole family were able to participate in the blessing and celebrate together.

Soon afterwards, house hunting began in earnest. After some initial viewings, we accepted an offer on our house and finalised the move towards Horsforth, some years later, after Finn was born. We continued with our walks to 'Donegal Pauline's' and back but stopped going for a while because Finn, in his 'terrible twos' caused havoc one day.

We rang the Holy Name Catholic Voluntary Academy and by luck or fate, a girl from that primary school class was leaving for Australia. I spoke to the Executive Head, Peter Hughes and explained Cara's health problems. He quickly approved Cara's application and the house move followed the next day.

It was organised chaos trying to sort school uniforms while the house was upside down with unpacked boxes. We soon settled into the home and school, and Finn was enjoying the nursery.

I remember how we were sitting in the garden on a warm summer day in June, listening to music and watching the red kites overhead. We discussed how fortunate we were to have made a house move to a better area and for Cara to finally have a brother. But we also had a gut feeling that something wasn't right and that something could be snatched from us. It just felt a bit too good to be true.

Brainstem Tumour Diagnosis

We attended a six-monthly hospital appointment at the chest clinic and met with a new Consultant. We explained how Cara was doing quite well at that stage but struggled to lie flat on the ground. During yoga exercises on her bedroom floor, she would sit upright in a panic, complaining about dizziness and nausea.

He decided to ask one of his colleagues in oncology for advice. Still, he did not seem particularly concerned about her balance, posture, and dizzy spells. Nevertheless, the MRI scan would clear things up.

As we left, he again tried to allay our fears by saying that it probably wasn't a neurological issue, but we should try to rule things out. Something didn't feel right, and I wondered a few times 'what if they find something?'

Two weeks later, the school closed for the summer holidays. Our holiday to Spain was approaching when the call came through. The message was that oncology would prefer an MRI scan before the holiday.

Our three-week holiday to Majorca was planned for August 2018 - two days after the proposed MRI scan. Our luggage was partially packed and almost ready to go.

Faye took Cara while I ventured down afterwards with Finn in his new black pushchair. After ringing the MRI scan number, I was told that Cara needed a second scan because of a technical error. A nurse then directed me to a separate ward.

I knew in my bones that something was amiss, and sprinted through the hospital corridors pushing Finn until we spotted Faye, who looked how I felt, shell-shocked. After a short wait in the side room, the Asian Consultant who initially referred Cara had arrived. I strolled out to the corridor and noticed that his demeanour had changed from the last visit.

Looking through me for a few seconds, he then broke the news that broke our hearts. Cara had been diagnosed with a brain tumour, and it was dire. It had infiltrated the brainstem and was one of the worst tumours, because of its impact and location. Darkness descended as we struggled to accept the scan results of this devastating and potentially life-threatening disease.

A brain tumour is a growth of cells in the brain that multiplies in a strange, uncontrollable way. Brain tumours are graded according to how fast they grow and how likely they are to grow back after treatment. Grade 1 and 2 tumours are low grade, and grade 3 and 4 tumours are high grade.

There are 2 main types of brain tumours: non-cancerous (benign) brain tumours– these are low grade (grade 1 or 2), which means they grow slowly and are less likely to return after treatment; and cancerous (malignant) brain tumours– these are high grade (grade 3 or 4) and either start in the brain (primary tumours) or spread into the brain from elsewhere (secondary tumours); they're more likely to grow back after treatment (11).

Cara and Finn sat quietly in the play area, watching television as we looked on, overwhelmed with shock. The Consultant Paediatric Neurosurgeon John Goodden visited us and explained the implications.

He planned to take a tumour sample the following morning and informed us that biopsies are high-risk procedures, especially with brainstem tumours. He asked if Cara knew and understood the seriousness of the disease. She did not! We described the tumour as a 'bump' to allay her fears.

John explained that if it was a high-grade tumour, then Cara would have a maximum life expectancy of 18 months. Conversely, if it was low grade (which was unlikely because of its location), then she could potentially live for 'many many years'. Those three words flashed through our minds relentlessly, as we clung to the hope that the tumour was not high grade.

We took Cara to a nearby restaurant later that night for a treat before returning to the hospital. We were distraught for Cara and could not understand why this was happening after everything that she had been through. Faye slept at the side while I snuggled in with Cara on her small single hospital bed where we prayed and hugged.

I struggled to console her throughout the night as she wept and frequently gripped my arms with worry. We were deeply concerned for her and could tell that her breathing was becoming laboured under the stress.

She continued fretting until drifting off to sleep at around 3am. Faye and I then went for a cup of tea in the parent's room, and there was one Glasgow Celtic cup, which Faye gave to me saying 'this must be a good-luck sign.'

We awoke to be surrounded by the medical team at 7am, who told us to prepare for surgery in the next 30 minutes. Poor Cara was mortified, asking if we were still going to Spain, and 'why is this happening to me again'?

The Asian doctor dropped by to wish us luck and to 'prepare for some hard roads ahead', which seemed like an omen. Looking back, we were so grateful for that initial scan because it gave us the opportunity for 18 months of beautiful memories.

We both walked Cara to the theatre. This time, she was a nervous wreck, so we were both invited into the pre-op holding room.

It was surreal and heart-wrenching watching Cara panic and cry, not understanding what was going on. Faye's folks took Finn, and we went home for a shower and change of clothes before getting the train from Horsforth back to town.

Waiting for the train to arrive, we both discussed how maybe this was God's plan – that we had taken her as far as we could and now it was in the Big Man's hands.

After the train arrived, we walked towards Park Row beside the Catholic cathedral. The phone rang around 2.15pm, and it was John (the surgeon).

My heart sank as he reminded me about the conversation yesterday – about how this was a high-risk operation, before saying that Cara's OK now, but something serious had happened during surgery.

An episode occurred as he moved onto the 6th sample of the tumour, which led to heart and blood pressure problems. She was then sent for a CT scan.

Upon our arrival at the High Dependency Unit, we noticed how Cara was exhausted and had a slight tick in her eye. The high dependency nurse remarked that a brainstem tumour was a terrible disease, and the one thing he particularly fears himself. Cara's Consultant John was relieved that the episode occurred when retrieving the last sample, and could now proceed to send for tests, with a one-to-two-week turnaround time for results. We asked his opinion, but he advised us to wait for the test results but to expect chemotherapy.

The next day, John dropped by and explained that these types of tumours are not cancer per-se, but Macmillan nurses would still see us. Waiting for the biopsy results was a terrifying experience. The Friday before my family arrived, Faye received a call from the oncology unit to say that the results were in.

The secretary could not discuss matters but gave us the option of a Tuesday, Wednesday, or Friday appointment. Tuesday it was, and so we began to surmise the potential scenarios - feeling fine one minute and sheer panic the next.

My sisters Donna and Carla heard about the healing properties of an old wooden Irish cross. After collecting it from Dundalk, they took it back to Belfast then across to Leeds on Saturday morning. I took Cara along for the ride to collect my mum and sisters from the airport.

She was feeling dizzy and unstable on her feet, requiring an arm to support her. Once the family arrived, we headed home and straight to Cara's room for prayers. They placed the cross under Cara's pillow where it would remain for the next two nights before returning it to its owner.

My brother Damien and his son Emmet arrived on a lunchtime flight. We then took a long walk to 'Donegal Pauline's' for some lunch. Pauline and her family knew Cara from birth, and Pauline's sister taught Cara at school. It was a weird and emotional afternoon as the potentiality of Tuesday's prognosis grew closer. Later that evening, we took the family to one of our local curry houses before returning home for a quiet night.

Knaresborough

Early the next morning, we visited Knaresborough by train – one of Cara's favourite spots just 30 minutes away from our home. The small medieval 'Chapel of Our Lady of the Crag' has been a place of sanctuary through Cara's ill health (12) tumours.

Dense wood, trees, shrubs, with plants and herbs lead a winding path to the altar. The only way to visit is to trail up narrow steps towards the small chapel area.

We often visited the chapel and prayed at the outside altar, which only opens to the general public on Sunday's from 2-4 pm. This is an old and quirky building which is carved directly into the rock (13).

It was built by 'John the Mason' in the early 1400s. John was working in the nearby quarry when he spotted a rock falling close to where his son was playing.

Because of the distance and speed of the rock, he couldn't physically intervene and instead prayed to the Virgin Mary. Miraculously his son was saved as the falling stones changed course during the prayer.

John thanked Our Lady and built the Chapel in appreciation for the miracle. Inside, includes a sculpted statue of Madonna and Child.

I remember taking a leaf from an herb plant and placing it on Cara's neck because it mentioned healing properties for the brain. After entering the Chapel, we lit a candle and prayed the rosary for Cara.

Afterwards, feeling tired and hungry, we visited Mother Shipton's Inn which is next to the nearby Mother Shipton's Cave, where a waterfall turns almost everything to stone. Many items, including bike wheels and boots, have accumulated over centuries and dangle at the entrance to the well.

> *[Mother Shipton] was born in a cave at Knaresborough. She foretold the future that included the Gunpowder Plot of 1605, the steam engine, aircraft or flying machines and even radio. She was Ursula Southiel, born in 1488 and died in 1561. The resident ghost at the Mother Shipton pub, with history from 1645, is Peggy, a gypsy. Stories abound that over the years, Peggy has tapped licensees on their shoulders, telling tales of woe. When she appears, she is dressed in layers of clothing, held about the waist by a piece of rope (14).*

On our visit, we sat looking onto the river on a beautiful sunny day, and all seemed to take strength from the visit to Knaresborough. Cara decided to fix Donna's hair. She loved to do French Plaits and was a little expert, but sometimes heavy-handed as Donna's face told a tale. We then strolled up to get fish and chips before returning to Leeds.

On Monday, my family returned to Ireland, and Cara's appointment was at 10am on Tuesday. As we arrived at the Oncology ward, we were shocked and saddened to see so many ill children.

These were impassive faces of young souls going through the rigours of chemo, radiation, or facing life-changing surgery. Parents and carers looked strained while trying to stay positive for their kids. We were the same, and I remember Cara asking why I was looking so worried.

We entered Dr Sue Picton's office and were amazed to see Carole Appleby, Cara's Tracheostomy nurse. Carole changed roles, but here she was again, still looking after Cara in a different capacity. We sat down in the three seats provided, and I then asked Dr Sue Picton directly if it was high grade or low grade. The relief was palpable when we found it to be low grade. Still, the level of detail, including location to the most sensitive part of the brainstem and potential risks brought us back to earth. But we always agreed that small wins should be celebrated.

Dr Sue Picton then informed us that Cara would avoid chemo for the moment because sometimes, the best option was to sit, watch and wait – with regular scans. Sometimes, these tumours can simply stop growing or grow away from the stem and cause less problems. But the wait and see approach meant that God answered our prayers. We asked God to just give us a chance, and that is what HE did. We joked that this news was even better than a three-week holiday and were surprised when the team suggested that there may not be an issue about travelling abroad after-all. Still, they would need to double-check with the team. Once confirmed, specialist travel insurance was acquired, before we booked the flights to Majorca. We were looking forward to meeting up with my brother, who was on the last few days of his holiday with his wife and son. We will treasure the memories of that trip forever.

Waterbaby

Cara loved swimming in the sea with me and Damien, who would bring his snorkel and stash of bread from the breakfast table and go fish hunting. She was a real water baby and loved splashing about. It was sad to see someone with airway problems unable to visit the swimmers when back in Leeds because of the effect of chlorine on her lungs.

On one rare occasion, I took her swimming in a local health club pool and bumped into an old friend Mike Tobin (Tobes), the owner of Tobins Muay Thai Boxing Gym in Leeds. I trained there for several years until shortly after Cara was born.

Tobes was in the pool with his son who was swimming with poise for such a young age. The family had a pool at their Portuguese villa, and he wanted to ensure that his kids could swim safely. I felt gutted for Cara as she watched the boy almost half her age swim like a torpedo.

We still had fun in the water, and she swam small sections of the pool, but I could tell that she was increasingly self-conscious. Tobes encouraged me to take Cara down to the gym for exercise sessions four years earlier.

I seriously considered doing so because of his record of training so many Thai boxing champions at different age levels. He was great at bringing younger kids from the streets through and giving them a focus in life through sport. But I worried about her cardiovascular problems and limited lung capacity, so she never made it down. Instead, we stuck to longer walks and lighter workouts at home.

Making The Most Of Life

After the diagnosis, we continued to travel and make the most of life. We flew to Belfast for Caodhan's christening (Kirsty and Conal's child).

My friend Dee took us straight to the hotel before telling us the plan: 'go and relax and I'll take the kids for a few hours'. It was hard to argue, so we dropped the bags off and went for a nice lunch to watch the United match.

Dee took them to see Bridgeen, and their kids Ryan, John, and Laura. Hours later, we heard the unmistakable voices of Cara, Finn and Laura before Cara crashed in through the door with presents galore. Dee took the kids on a shopping trip and treated them to boxes of presents. Cara's face was a picture.

Cara also got to spend some time with Joan and Gerry Senior in November 2018. Gerry Senior was a very religious man. His health deteriorated over the years, but Cara was always in his prayers. Still joking and smiling, even in the last stages of his life as he battled a terrible disease.

A month later, (New Year's Eve), we were on route from Leeds to Belfast. Thirty minutes into the short flight, my phone rang which seemed strange because it was in flight mode. Carla's number appeared, so I switched the power off completely. We just knew. Upon arrival, the SMS confirmed that Gerry Senior had died. We were gutted and wanted to have one last bit of quality time with him and Joan. 2019 would also be Cara's last New Year.

Throughout the MRI scans and various health problems, we continued to make the most of life. I was glad to hear that the Manchester United legends were due to play Bayern Munich legends in a charity match. We booked a hotel and match tickets and jumped on the early morning train from Leeds. Cara had a United scarf, but we couldn't convince Faye, the Leeds United supporter, to wear one.

Cara relished the match experience. It was a great family day out. We took the tram to the stadium and bought hotdogs for the kids at half time. United was going through a period of transition, and it was great to see the United players of old putting on a show.

The players might have aged, but their quality was still evident. We finished the night at a Thai restaurant, and the kids loved sitting in the 'tuk-tuk' (Thai taxi vehicle) and sipping mocktails. Later that summer, we enjoyed a belated wedding anniversary and took the kids on trips to York.

On one occasion, as we approached York train station, we noticed a wasp flying around the carriage. Faye then felt something in her hair. Placing a hand behind her right ear, she realised it was moving.

It stung her neck, just behind the earlobe, before she flung it against the window. We discussed how the sting was located around the site of Cara's tumour (behind the ear) and wondered if this was a sign.

A similar thing happened while I jogged past St Mary's Catholic Church in Horsforth. As I was looking towards the statue of Our Lady, a wasp hit the back of my neck at lightning speed as I asked Mary to watch over Cara.

York was swarming with tourists, as we walked down to the Shambles. We then spotted the entrance to the small Catholic church (St Margaret's) and took the kids in for a quick prayer. The little Roman Catholic Church of St Margaret Clitherow contains a shrine. We had walked past this church so many times but did not realise it existed.

Widely recognised as a Martyr for the Catholic faith, Margaret was born in the city of York in 1556. Fifteen years later, after marrying a local, wealthy butcher, John Clitherow, she converted to Catholicism in 1574 (15).

Preaching or sheltering a priest from the authorities in England was seen as an act of treason. Same for Catholic priests in Ireland who often performed mass in secret, in locations such as Ardara in Donegal.

Margaret had Mass celebrated above the family's house and shop in the Shambles. She also ran a small school to teach the Catholic faith to children. In 1586 her activities were betrayed to the authorities. When charged, Margaret refused to plead. She did not want to expose her family, friends or the children in her school to the risks involved in giving evidence in a trial: they may have betrayed others; they might have denied their faith in public.

The penalty for refusing to plead was being crushed to death. It was expected that the victim, in the absence of other evidence, might betray herself under the torture. Margaret suffered this fate on 25th March 1586. It was Good Friday and the Feast of the Annunciation. She prayed aloud but gave nothing away (16).

Faye felt a cold breeze drift past when praying at the front of the church. She quickly turned, surprised not to see Cara or Finn behind her. They were standing at the back of the aisle alongside me. Faye believes that someone or something had crossed her path in that tiny church.

Cara then sat with her legs hanging over the small ledge at the back of the church and wrote something in the visitor book. We returned a year later to find that the church had been closed during the pandemic.

Fortunately, we contacted the local priest who emailed a picture of Cara's note. She had asked people to:

"Pray for the world, family, friends, and my future health."

Donegal Family Holiday

My brother Damien lent us his small red Nissan car for a summer trip to Donegal in July 2019. After a late-night visiting family in Belfast, we grabbed the keys, packed small suitcases into the car and drove off in the misty Irish rain to Donegal. Damien's car had been around a few corners alright, and from various tales, seen almost every inch of Ireland.

Damien, Barry, Norney, Skilly and his mates from Beechmount would go on their adventures around the island of Ireland with tents, surfboards, and abundant supplies.

Driving to Donegal that morning, Cara wasn't impressed by the lack of luxury and moaned throughout – begging me to park up and hire a car. Approximately five miles from Ardara, as the heavens opened, we heard an almighty smash. The car rocked as if it had been blasted by a rocket. One of the wipers broke, and condensation steamed the windows. It seemed like part of the engine had collapsed but I was determined to trail onto Ardara.

The torrential rain made for harsh driving conditions as we pulled into the main street. Grabbing the suitcases and kids, we whizzed over the road and into the comfort of our hotel.

Within minutes we were in our room, and I was straight on the phone, giving my brother grief about the car. He was convinced that there was nothing wrong with the car and would drive up the next day and prove it.

Next morning, we stepped outside the hotel to check the car after my brother had arrived. Damien meticulously checked the engine but there was no sign of damage.

Maybe we caught some debris which stuck under the car and trailed? So that, plus the driving conditions may have combined to make us believe that the vehicle had almost combusted.

The kids loved Donegal, and the food was fantastic. The freshest seafood in Nancy's bar, and the finest meats and vegetables from the land. Being a food lover, Cara was in her element. We drove up a high mountainside, with enough space for barely one car.

Following Damien, Jacqui, and Emmet in the vehicle in front, we were confronted with sheep as the clutch almost burnt out, such was the steepness.

Looking over my left shoulder, I had a vision of the car conking out and us having to push the little car over the side of the mountain before piling into the jeep in front.

Damien, Cara, and I jumped into the sea in our wetsuits before having a BBQ on the beach. After visiting a beautiful waterfall, we bid farewell and drove to Bundoran.

We visited Bundoran throughout our childhood to escape the troubles over the 12th July and the Orange marching season. It brought back incredible memories, and our kids loved it—great craic ('good times', especially in Ireland) at the amusements during the day, then Irish music sessions in the evening.

We visited a fascinating restaurant that initially reminded us of Fawlty Towers TV show but was actually the complete opposite. The kids really liked its charm and were amazed at the quality of the food. Later, Faye won a furry dog with pink sequin love hearts on its collar at the amusements. Cara was over the moon, and her smile in the picture was something else. Our trip to Donegal was even more special because she was carefree and back to her old self again: a big happy kid.

Turf Lodge Faith Healer

When we returned to Belfast, Donna had heard about a faith healer from the Turf Lodge area. Cara visited this man with my mother and my sisters that afternoon.

After some prayers, he turned and warned them that evil was always lurking. Jumping quickly in shock, the faith healer asked if someone put a tack on the passenger seat of the car?

He then used this example to explain the good versus evil connection in more detail. As God's children, we have the capacity and capability to accept that adverse events are an inescapable part of the human condition and a fact of life. He encouraged our family to keep the faith. They were stunned when he said confidently 'this child will never need chemo'.

My youngest sister Carla had a kidney transplant in recent years and afterwards, fell ill with lymphoma. Thankfully, she recovered after a rigorous 6-month bout of treatment. It was upsetting to see Carla in such pain and discomfort. The loss of her hair was a real physical reminder of the rigours of treatment.

Our daughter Cara loved her own dark, brown shiny hair, and we dreaded the thought of her going through a similar experience to her aunt Carla. It soon became apparent that God had other plans.

It was our last night in Belfast with family and friends, so we decided to visit the Failte Restaurant for our last family meal. Damien's mate Skilly treated the family to bottles of wine at the restaurant.

Great food and great company. Cara was busy tucking into a massive burger, surrounded by her loving cousins. This would be her final trip to Ireland.

One final trip to my mum's house to bid farewell and we were gone. My sisters and mum often mention how Cara gave them the biggest cuddle as she left.

MRI Scans

After returning from a summer holiday in Cala D'or, it became increasingly apparent that the stress and strain of the brain tumour were taking its toll on Cara and the family. We made the best of our time with Cara and were conscious about the pending MRI scan.

My colleague, Professor Becky Malby, referred to the tumour as a 'ticking time bomb'. She wondered if hormones and age could influence the tumour. In hindsight, she may have been right. Becky and I also discussed the lack of empirical knowledge about brainstem tumours.

Cara tended to fret more after her 11th birthday and gradually developed a problem with her balance and swallowing food.

Faye and I continued to call the brain tumour a 'bump'. We tried to desensitise her to it while explaining that lots of people have bumps without realising it.

I found it difficult to read into the ramifications of brainstem tumours, and instead sought advice from people with direct professional or family experience.

We often discussed the topic with our neighbours, Chris, and Emma. Chris had a background in tumour research and would put our minds at ease by explaining medical advances and suggesting reasons to be hopeful. However, he often advised us to push for its removal, even if its growth had stunted.

I remember one conversation with an old friend 'Dan' who mentioned how our other mate (also Dan) had a family member with a similar tumour.

Dan and I later discussed this, and I remember feeling cheered when he described how his cousin had a 'tumour the size of a tennis ball removed from the base of his skull 30 years ago and was now flying – and doing great'. All we craved was a chance.

Cara did not mind undertaking MRI scans, but I couldn't enter the scan room. Part of a sewing needle remains lodged in my left foot from Belfast, 1985. Faye accompanied her to each twelve-week scan, but the build-up to the results was mentally draining for everyone, especially Cara.

At Christmas, 2018, the doctors gave us what seemed like a perfect result. No sign of change and fortunately, she transitioned from three to six-monthly scans.

If that next scan showed a similar outcome, there was the potential for being moved onto yearly scans which for us would be as good as it could get. We became much more relaxed and happier after being given this ray of hope. Maybe it was not going to be as bad as what it seemed.

Dr Sue Picton (oncologist) and John Goodden (neurosurgeon) met with us in June 2019 to discuss the latest scan results. Our initial optimism dissipated when John described how the tumour had grown by 4mm in 12 months.

Another 4mm on the brainstem would start to affect the brainstem function, and so he would 'bet [his] mortgage' on Cara needing surgery by Christmas, 2019.

The follow-up meeting took place after the six-month MRI scan. It was not what we were expecting, and Cara's mood darkened. John discussed the pros-and-cons of surgery, but the details were difficult to digest.

The conversation shifted from stunting the tumour after excising it, to potential loss of sight, cardiac arrest, or brain haemorrhage. There was also the reality that 'she may not wake up'.

Poor Cara broke down, and Carole, the Macmillan nurse described her 'like a little girl again, so innocent and scared'. To say that Faye and I were worried was an understatement.

Our approach was to treat every day uniquely, and if it ever came to further surgery or chemo, then we would prefer to tell Cara shortly beforehand.

She was normally a little dreamer but shook like a sparrow and grew increasingly agitated as the enormity of the prognosis sunk in.

We were deeply appreciative of the team at the LGI, including the neurologist and oncologist who were terrific, and who explained the next step: an MRI at the end of August with potential surgery on 22nd September 2019.

If it somehow did not grow, then the following scan would take place in December 2019 or January 2020. We were distraught for Cara but decided to keep things as normal as possible. Purchasing a new high school uniform, and new school and exercise bags cheered her up.

The plan was for Cara to at least start and experience high school. Still the summer holidays, so we booked another holiday in Majorca because the kids loved the weather, swimming coves, food, and activities.

At our hotel in Cala Egos, we would treat the kids to late-afternoon milkshakes and potatoes bravas whilst we sat with a drink before making our way past the yachts at the Cala D'or marina. We took a mini train and a boat trip that visited various beaches and resorts.

When the boat ride ended, the heat was so intense that we all jumped into the clear blue seawater and had a great time. Cara wasn't a great swimmer but was improving and asked me to walk her to the cliff-edge where the other kids were jumping into the sea below.

After walking her up, she grew panicky after realising that the drop was about 15 feet in height. Not wanting to worry her, I calmly walked her back to the cove where she continued to watch in awe at the other kids jumping.

This time I suggested that we go together, hold hands, and jump together. After some initial trepidation, we stood on the ledge. Once I said, 1,2 3 – we jumped through the roasting Majorcan air and into the lush calm sea below.

I immediately turned to lift Cara because I knew that she would panic underwater. But the look of accomplishment on her face was fantastic.

She had the most beautiful smile and gave me a massive hug. We will return someday and do that jump again and drop her ashes into the cove that she loved.

Upon our return to Leeds, the MRI scan took place in August, but the results came through when we were in London. Dr Sue Picton agreed to set up a video call for the following week which suggested grounds for optimism. Usually, we would visit the oncology ward in person, so maybe things were not so bad after all.

That night, we were heading towards the West End and bumped into a Belfast woman and her little girl. The child had significant visual impairment and had just arrived by air ambulance.

 After asking for directions, we chatted and discussed Cara. We gave the child a small gift before both families wished each other well. A timely reminder that many other kids were on the same boat.

Cardinal Heenan High School

Cara started Cardinal Heenan High School (17) at the start of September 2019. We were probably more nervous than she was on her first day. She looked beautiful and so grown up as we took pictures before she left for the school bus.

The following day, we attended Finn's opening day at Cara's old primary school followed by a video clinic meeting with Dr Sue Picton. After asking how Cara was doing, she told us that the tumour had not grown, and if we were happy with Cara in general (which we were), then the next MRI would be in three to four months.

During November 2019, Cara became increasingly panicky when eating. We wondered if this was linked to a previous choking episode at an Indian restaurant. This was during a small family celebration held because her eye examination was encouraging. She continued to struggle with simple tasks, like crossing the road or getting in and out of elevators which were causing panic.

By the end of November, she began to complain about occasional headaches, described as a dull ache as she was, e.g. rushing to get dressed for school or running for the bus.

It was fun and games each morning just getting her ready and out for school. She did not show any signs of seizures (fits) (although she had some sort of an episode when we found her that fateful night after biting through her tongue).

Neither was there mention of nausea, vomiting or drowsiness, but we noticed the growing mental and behavioural changes. We often called her 'Cara five-times' (needing to be asked for something more than once) which amused her.

There were also personality changes, where she increasingly became agitated at the most mundane things which were so disheartening to witness. Cara was such a beautiful and gentle soul, who cared deeply about her friends and best friend (Sarah-Jane) and family.

She was conscious of the tumour effects while still grappling with war wounds from past operations. These stemmed from reconstructive surgery which left deep scars on her throat and chest.

So, our hearts were breaking to see Cara go into her shell and increasingly hide from the world at a time when she should have been enjoying high school. Still, she was also blissfully happy in her own little world surrounded by family and friends who she loved dearly.

Cara's Last Christmas

Reality kicked in when the MRI scan date arrived. 23rd December 2019. We immediately contacted Carole and the team to ask if it would be safe to request a change of appointment until the first week in January 2020.

John rescheduled the potential surgery date until 16th January 2020 (the subsequent day of Cara's funeral). The sweet feeling of victory was ours. Surgery was a distinct possibility, so it was essential for Cara to have the most peaceful and enjoyable Christmas possible.

In the weeks leading up to Christmas, we tried to lift Cara's spirits as she came home each day from school. Cara had low self-esteem and could not get her head around social media and the way, some kids behaved.

She took every word for granted, good-and-bad, and I often told her to hit the ball back. 'If someone says something to offend you, then just respond in kind'. But she struggled with the politics of life as an 11-year-old and never felt like 'one of the cool kids' as she described them.

Cara initially believed in Santa (Father Christmas) but like many kids at that age, increasingly doubted his existence. She often asked, 'What's the point in Christmas if there's no Santa?' Because of her health concerns, and knowing how much she loved Christmas, we had a chat, and I told her that there was a Saint Nicholas.

I advised her to read into the story of Saint Nicholas, who dressed in a red suit at Christmas time many centuries ago and gave generously to the poor and vulnerable. I also sent her a WhatsApp link narrating the story of St Nicholas.

When we next spoke, she said 'Dad. I get it, so it's like the way some people believe in fairies, and some don't', and I said 'exactly'. Finally, her spirits were lifted. She momentarily returned to that big happy child again by buzzing around the house and finally joining into the Christmas spirit.

A loud rap on Christmas Eve had the kids running to answer the door. They screamed when Cara spotted two boxes on the doorstep. Inside were small toys and chocolates. Faye asked Cara to keep the boxes safe for use the following year.

We then walked to St Mary's Chapel for Christmas Eve Mass. Cara's school mates and teachers were in the packed congregation. We then stopped at the chippy for a snack.

Cara tucked into a pile of gluten-free onion rings as we strolled home. In no time, they were both in their pyjamas and giddy to see the treats (carrots, mince pies and milk) for Santa beneath the tree.

I then told Cara and Finn that a secret message from Santa had just arrived. We all gathered around the computer in my study with the lights out, as the short clip began *'Hellooooo Cara, I'm Santa. I'm with my elves here...I hear you have a brother called Finn, etc.'*.

Cara's face beamed with joy, but she seemed to hyperventilate with excitement. We kept reminding her to breathe, but she went hyper.

Midway through the video message, she frantically pulled out her phone to record the clip, but her hands were shaking with delight. She was determined to send the clip to her best friend, Sarah-Jane.

The look on her face and the atmosphere in the room was fantastic and something that we will never forget. Age was catching up with her in the context of believing in 'Santa'. But we managed to prescribe her with some magic after all.

Christmas Day at Faye's family home was great. Cara claimed the front seat of her Grandad's jeep going to -and-from our home. Boxing Day was also great craic.

Mike and Becky and their kids joined Faye's folks and sister Lucy at ours for another turkey dinner. I remember washing up at 11pm and singing while Cara sauntered about looking for more chocolate. We both laughed together. I finally put her to bed, and off she went to sleep after a long day.

The next day, 27th December, Cara sorted through her Christmas presents and new clothes, and we went to a local pizza restaurant and took a short walk around Kirkstall Abbey to clear our heads. On December 28th, we started to prepare for the joint New Year's Eve celebrations and a birthday trip to Ireland but were concerned when Cara mentioned about feeling unwell.

She did not seem 100%, so we cancelled the planned sleepover at their grandparents that night. It wasn't worth risking a night out then losing a trip to Ireland if she deteriorated. So instead, we stayed at home and began to get organised for our trip to Ireland.

Cara's Last Meal

Finn had chills and a runny nose for a while over the Christmas period, but that was usual for wintertime. We didn't overthink it. Later that night of the 28th December, Cara started to complain about aches and chills and was not feeling any better. Faye called me to the bathroom because she noticed that her complexion had changed. Still, when I arrived, it returned to normal. Slightly unstable on her feet, we linked up and walked her to bed.

We watched the Manchester United match downstairs, as Faye and Finn took turns to drop by her room. They laughed when she asked why the fuss? And why were they checking up on her? She was 'trying to chill' in front of the bedroom television.

Her condition improved as the night progressed and late in the evening, I brought a small plate of Indian food to her room to check if she had any appetite. Within a split second, she made a beeline for her pillows to support her back and jumped upright, saying 'yes please' with a smile on her face. Little did I know that the chicken saag, rice and chapati would be her last supper.

Faye checked in with her again at 9.30pm. Cara was in a deep sleep, and Finn was asleep in his bed. Around midnight, we both individually checked on Cara. We then went to bed, content that she looked and sounded fine.

At 3am, a strange cracking noise stemmed from her bedroom, but considering her frequent bouts of sleep apnoea, I was more reassured rather than worried. A few hours later, I awoke again and felt a strange sensation in our cold dark room.

An eerily silence pervaded as I strolled to the bathroom, then, as usual, would check on Cara before returning to bed. In the darkness of her room, I noticed that she was positioned sidewise on the bed with both legs dangling. After grabbing her foot, my heart sank as I realised that it was ice cold. Moving my hand up her freezing leg, I then quickly felt her face and realised that she was in trouble.

I screamed for Faye, and within seconds the light was on, as the battle to put some semblance of life into her chilled limbs and organs began. Her pale skin and hauntingly beautiful green eyes looked out of place as we took turns to perform mouth-to-mouth and chest compressions. The 15-minute wait for an ambulance felt like an eternity as we begged her not to leave us.

Finn stood at the end of the bed watching things unfold before saying calmly that 'Cara's gone, Daddy, she's away to heaven'.

As I climbed into the front seat of the ambulance, the driver appeared. He slipped the seatbelt on and pulled out of the street, before mumbling in a soft and caring voice, 'I'm sorry to tell you this, but I doubt that your daughter will be alive when we arrive at the hospital'. I immediately asked if he had any kids himself, before remarking that I hope he never has to experience anything like this in his lifetime. It is the worst day of my life. I told him to enjoy every minute with them because he will never get it back when it is gone.

At the hospital, I sat in shock and silence as a large team congregated around Cara. They kept looking down the corridor at me, before calling me in and informing me that there was nothing else that they could do. That she had been dead for a while.

As I strolled in, head bowed and shaking in disbelief, here was my little Leeds Irish rose laid out gracefully on the hospital bed, now passed to the other side. I shared some moments with her, reminiscing and praying as I kissed her beautiful pale skin - never wanting to release her.

Faye and her Dad appeared, and all three us took turns to kiss and hug our precious girl. Later, the doctor called us to a side room consisting of a senior Consultant, detective, and other doctors to walk through events leading to Cara's death.

Soon afterwards, discussions about morgues, autopsies and funeral arrangements quickly dominated discussions instead of trips to Belfast and Dublin for family celebrations.

Finding Cara was the stuff of horrors and something that we will take to our graves. But from the darkness came a light as we were soon to be transported into a world of magic – of orbs, angels, and holy ghosts.

Note From Uncle Damien

Comforting words from my brother after Cara's passing.

For ye yourselves are fully aware that the day of the Lord will come like a thief in the night. That is how Cara was taken. She went to bed and never woke up. It was late December, just after Christmas when our family usually heads away somewhere for a few nights to wind down after the Christmas rush. We visited Ardara on the West Coast of Ireland. To Nancy's Bar for pints of porter and big bowls of fresh mussels, amid the howling gales and mercurial weather patterns on the Atlantic's edge.

Our usual room was occupied, so the landlady gave us the adjacent apartment. Settling in on our arrival, an uneasy feeling came upon me. The room was spacious. Black pillows adorned the sofa. Black feathers on the pillows were discarding and falling to the floor. They reminded me of death, darkness and an old Irish film called Darby O'Gill and the Little People (18).

In the film, a black funeral horse pulled up by a home to remove a body. Black feathers were decorated on the horse's face. I visited the bathroom and as the light shone upon the curtains, it resembled a black funeral veil. I told Jacqui how this place made me feel uneasy before we left for Nancy's Bar. Jacqui remarked how she was texting Faye and how Cara had a slight temperature but would be keeping an eye on her.

Around 5.40am the following morning, my phone rang. It was a WhatsApp call, and the background light showed that it was Kieran. I let it ring, hoping that he had rang by mistake. Jacqui wondered if he was ringing about my mum and then Kieran rang back to tell us that Cara was dead.

There was no use trying to enquire. Kieran was lost in a world of pain and a grey, dystopian nightmare. I tried to offer him comfort but no words can console after losing his daughter. The conversation ended around 5.41am. The call lasted just under a minute – as quickly as our Cara's life ended. She had gone to heaven at only 11 years of age.

Faye and Kieran met at Liverpool University and then he moved to Leeds - Faye's hometown. After settling down and pursuing more academia, they tried for a bambino. Low and behold, within a short period of time, Cara was born. Years later, we made a surprise trip to Leeds and went straight to collect Cara from respite.

She appeared in the hallway looking dazed and tired. She did a double-take – looked at me and then her dad; then back and forth as she hadn't seen me in a year before the penny dropped. She realised it was her Uncle Damien but struggled to talk. Her voice was obstructed by the Tracheostomy tube, but she gave me a smile that would melt a heart of stone.

When she was decannulated, I remember her happy self at my mum's house with a beautiful cheerful voice, running up and down the stairs with red rosy cheeks and dollop of dark hair. She loved her food; she loved her family; she loved travelling to Ireland, and she loved life.

In July 2019, we all met in Donegal: Kieran and his family and me with mine. We visited a secluded little beach. It was picture-postcard material. The aroma was of turf burning and the salty sea air literally took your breath away.

I gave Cara and Kieran wetsuits and the look on Cara's face when we told her how to warm up before jumping into the sea was legendary.

She looked horrified. But it was mesmerising watching her play in the cold Atlantic surf while Faye and Jacqui cooked food on a small BBQ nearby.

After 'a hAon, a Dó, a Trí' (1,2 3 in Irish) – we each took Cara by one hand before leaping into the water. It was a blast of a day before Kieran packed up and took Faye and the kids onto Bundoran.

Next time we saw Cara was at the Chapel of Rest in Leeds General Infirmary. Still in her PJs. How we all wish things were different. Cara suffered more than most kids her age, but her zest for life was sky high.

Kieran said to me during the wake that Cara was too gentle for this world. That she was missed sorely but was in a better place. I gave him a brotherly hug and said: 'God comfort you'.

Chapter 2 ~ Black is the Colour

Black is the Colour: 'Cara's Song'

Cara enjoyed listening to stories from our travels. We often discussed our teaching escapades at a Hagwon in South Korea, journeys through SE Asia and wedding in Cuba.

Faye and I were married in Havana before Cara was born. Staff stocked the hotel fridge every morning with cava, soft drinks, and Cuban beer.

Each day, we packed our bag full of drinks and clothes and passed it to staff living in a large outbuilding that resembled an aircraft carrier at the back of the hotel.

We were surprised to learn that the team of hotel workers were living, eating, and sleeping in a hidden area almost adjacent to the luxury of a hotel resort.

Each day, the workers cheered in appreciation as the drink was shared, between the smiling, thirsty faces.

It was the same routine every day. The gardeners, cleaners, beach security guards and cooks enjoyed the gifts and appreciated the gesture. We often saw the ground staff with our hats, tops or my Gaelic football shirts which was great to see.

We travelled alone to Cuba without family and friends. Luckily, we met a great group of people from Ireland and Scotland, who became the wedding party. Mick agreed to walk Faye down the aisle on her fathers' behalf while his wife Órlaith supported us and arrived early on the day of the wedding with champagne. Órlaith did Faye's hair while Mick and I had a singsong (an Irish wedding tradition) over a few drinks. Later that afternoon, in the searing heat, I serenaded Faye with 'Black is the Colour' after the wedding prayers. This song by Hamish Imlach was a Christy Moore favourite, which we sang many times during Cara's life and ultimately in death (19).

Black is the Colour of My True Love's Hair
Her Lips Are Like Some Roses Fair
She Has the Sweetest Smile and the Gentlest Hands
And I Love the Ground Whereon She Stands

I Love My Love and Well She Knows;
I Love the Ground Whereon She Goes
I Wish the Day It Soon Would Come
When She and I Could Be as One

I Go the Clyde and I Mourn and Weep
For Satisfied I Never Can Be
I Write Her a Letter, Just a Few Short Lines
And Suffer Death a Thousand Times

Black is the Colour of My True Love's Hair
Her Lips Are Like Some Roses Fair
She Has the Sweetest Smile and the Gentlest Hands
And I Love the Ground Whereon She Stands

Christy Moore poignantly mentioned how: 'This was one of Hamish's big songs. Every time I sing it, he is sitting beside me, I loved him dearly, still do'. Who would have thought that the song would be sung in darker circumstances, several years later?

This time, my family from Ireland and I were gathered around Cara at the morgue in Leeds, singing the same beautiful song. We then kissed and hugged her before saying our goodbyes.

A specialist team transferred Cara's body to Jimmy's hospital morgue where an amazing lady took over and cared beautifully for Cara.

She washed her hair and dressed her in a new pair of pyjamas purchased by the morgue team. A month earlier, Faye had bought the same pyjamas for Cara – what a coincidence.

Days later would be our final visit to the Chapel of Rest, where we hugged and kissed her ice-cold forehead. I

I then stroked her beautiful dark hair before gently rubbing a drop of coffee onto her soft lips. Her caffeine intake was restricted due to airway problems, so it was my little way of sharing something precious before departing. I know she will have smiled down on me.

Our Very Own Angel?

Our first day out as a family of three, just two weeks after Cara's death, felt overwhelming, as we strolled around Roundhay Park in Leeds. The sense of loss dawned as we took pictures of Finn hugging a tree and just wished that Cara was on the other side, hugging back. Later that night, we lit the candle given to us in a grief box by the parents of another deceased child. After praying in Irish, and having a yarn about Cara, Finn blew the candle out, and we moved back to the living room. It was just then that Faye noticed a light blue orb moving slowly across the ceiling.

Not believing her eyes, she called us over to observe the moving image. We were witnessing something so magical that it seemed to resemble the movie 'Finding Nemo'.

A sea of orbs of different sizes, shapes and colours appeared and started playing and spinning around the room, with some landing on Finn's face. In those minutes, we were distracted like big kids, following the orbs on their little adventures. At one point, Finn shouted 'they're in the kitchen'. Upon opening the kitchen door, two beautiful blue spheric shaped objects hovered a few feet above my head and a few feet apart, in the darkness.

We stood and watched in awe as they spun for a few seconds. One orb floated towards the kitchen window while the other flew directly at my face. Finn shouted: 'they hit my daddy on the head'.

When they gradually disappeared, we sat down in disbelief. We realised that something spiritual had just happened and started to suspect that we had our very own 'angel.

123

Spioraid Naoimh: Holy Ghosts

The spherical, ball-shaped objects which people refer to as orbs are unique, and just seeing them float in real-time is a sight to behold. They frequently appear on their own but occasionally as a rainbow of different colours (See Exhibit A and A* at www.ismisecara.com).

On one occasion, just before the first Covid-19 lockdown, we had a bizarre experience when dining at a busy restaurant in Horsforth, Leeds.

Faye took a picture of us both at the same table where Cara and Finn would often sit (Exhibit B on www.ismisecara.com).

We were reminiscing about Cara and feeling a bit low when flickers of light started to surround us after Faye took the picture.

Upon viewing the image, we were amazed to see a completely distorted picture of us both, beneath a hologram of lights, showering us with what appeared to be sparks.

Faye then took another snap, this time with my phone camera to ensure it wasn't a technical glitch, and again – were showered with a rainbow of beautiful light-rays. The image reminded us of something which we couldn't immediately fathom.

Weeks later, when standing at the back of Sunday morning mass, for the first time without Cara, Faye stared at the holy picture of Jesus directly facing us.

She then walked slowly towards it, pointing out its likeness to the restaurant picture. I knew immediately what she meant. We couldn't believe it. It seemed like the jigsaw was starting to make sense and that Cara was somehow reaching out to us.

Before Cara died, we had never seen the face of a single soul. Yet the sight of countless faces began to pop up in different locations. The faces of souls were becoming so voluminous that it seemed that literally scores appeared at any one time, no matter where we were.

I often wondered if it was my Granny and Grandad Mervyn who lived in Shiels Street behind the old Beehive pub. Both died before I was born. Or maybe my Aunts and Uncles Danny and Monica; Gerry and Dolores; or Hetty and Rosh and their dogs (animals appeared too).

Or friends who died young and in tragic circumstances. Just as likely, they might have been souls from my mother's side – an extremely religious family including my Grandad Malachy, Granny Lily, and her sisters Mary and Mena.

Mary (pronounced Mury) died in January 2020. My mum told me how Mary prayed through the night with no sleep when Cara went through tracheal surgery for subglottic stenosis. She was always smiling and never downbeat nor had a bad word to say about anyone.

Or might they be a mix of souls and include Faye's family who were a combination of Scottish and Welsh descendants. Like my granny Sarah Mervyn, Faye's grandmother Margaret was also very religious. We were glad that Margaret got to meet Cara before she died. The same for her great grandmother Irene from her mum's strand of the family.

Initially, we never felt threatened by the visitors to our home, but gradually became more alarmed. Still, we often wondered why and what the messages entailed?

Orbs and the spirit world are a topic that has fascinated people throughout the ages. From what we have gathered, it's a complex and contradictory subject area with no simple answer and is associated with spirits – both good and bad.

The origin of the term Holy Ghost, Holy Spirit or 'Spioraid Naomh' in Gaelic stems from the Hebrew words ruah ha-Godesh. 'Ruah' refers to breath, regarding the breath of our Lord, 'God'. It also correlates to air and wind.

> *I believe that the breath of life went into man's nostrils and is located over and throughout the brain giving us life. Hence, the Halo is over the head, representing the Holy Spirit giving us life. And without the breath of life, the brain would not function, and we would have no life in this world. The breath of life is connected to our spirits by the silver cord. When the silver cord is loosed, we are cut off from the breath of life, the brain dies, we become disconnected from our bodies, and are no longer part of this physical world (20).*

We are both quite curious about the spirit world. As kids, we would share ghost stories about wailing banshees [Bean Sí] or the fairy women spirits in Irish mythology. The story goes that a Bean Sí buzzes around the house on a mission. Anyone unfortunate enough to have heard her wail or witness a comb thrown, will subsequently perish.

We understand how critics may question the events that we have witnessed since Cara passed and may argue for an empirical evidence base.

127

Still, we feel that the pictures and videos captured over recent months disproves the theory that the orbs are a figment of our imagination. Or are nothing more than flickers of light, camera flashes or insects captured in motion.

These visitors often appear after praying, and usually at places where we have witnessed unexplainable phenomenon – at the sites of the supernatural and paranormal activity.

After almost daily discussions and reflections on these experiences, we realise that it's ongoing for a reason and orbs are only part of the picture. But why the different colours and what do they mean in practice?

From January 2020, we have been intrigued by the presence and colour of the different orbs. We believe that they relate to different energy colours.

Of course, there is no definite proof of what these orbs mean in practice. Interpretations may refer to the way one perceives the world, their religious background, or spiritual beliefs.

We, as a family, take a purely mindful approach to their explanation because the orbs seem to reflect our mood at any given time.

We recognise that some may be reading this and thinking that the colours are meaningless.

Others may believe that a holy ghost or another spirit type may be trying to pass on a message through a certain colour.

Mum's Dream

The autopsy process began, and we expected a long wait for the funeral and a longer wait for the post-mortem results. At first, we refused the option to receive Cara's body without her brain, which went for further tests. We felt that she had undergone so much surgery in her short life, so the body should be repatriated, in full. Our decision delayed the funeral by almost three weeks.

During this time, we reflected on two events (my mother's dream and a visit from a priest). Just as we were discussing the importance of organ donation, my mother (Marie) called on the Monday week before the funeral. She described her dream from the night before.

She was with Cara, and in a clear and robust voice, Cara advised: 'Granny, please remember that the brain is not the soul'. Just then, my mother awoke and scribbled the dream on paper as a reminder.

On the Thursday before the funeral (January 9th, 2020), the Coroners letter arrived which explained that the current cause of death was unexplained.

As we read through, Faye remarked that the place of birth and death were at the same hospital. Emotions were running high when we realised that Faye had given birth to Cara at the same place where she died 11 years later. We were then startled by a loud knock at the door.

A young priest called after serving mass at Cara's school 'Cardinal Heenan Catholic High School' for the teachers and her classmates. It was perfect timing and almost felt like Cara had sent him because we were feeling so low.

We visited Cara's room and prayed for a few moments before discussing the brain repatriation issue. The priest quickly put our minds at rest by saying precisely the same words as my mother about the brain and soul. The relief was palpable.

Shortly afterwards, on route to collecting Finn from primary school, we noticed white feathers lining the walk, every few feet to the school and back. We felt uplifted and finally accepted that the spirit had departed the body. Hence the decision to conduct the funeral ASAP.

Cara's Funeral

We visited Father Emmanuel at the parochial house in Leeds, to discuss the order of service and choose the prayers and songs. Over the previous days, we had worked on poems and the obituary, and Faye mentioned to the priest how she wrote a poem but hadn't the courage to speak in front of a packed church:

> 'You arrived so soon to shock us all; we really weren't expecting you that soon at all. We took you home you cried so loud; you shocked us into running around. You loved your food; you were the best; you'd try everything and then eat the rest. I know you're looking down on me, asking for a Yorkshire cup of tea. Your take on hair was unique; those French Plaits were a treat. Oh, Cara, I miss your gentle smile; and long dark hair with eyes so green and skin so fair. But now it's time to say goodbye, but not for good. Can't wait until we meet again, and I'll give you a hug'.

The priest was confident that Cara would give Faye the strength to read the poem. He was a force of calm amidst the grief and guided us magnificently throughout the process.

The day before the funeral, Sarah (Cara's friend's mum) noticed two white doves fly over our home, which we took as a symbol that Cara was at peace.

I lay on Cara's bed for a while before driving to collect my sister Sarah, brother-in-law Gerry, and friends Dee and Bridgeen from Leeds Bradford Airport. Feeling down just a few minutes earlier, I was now glad to meet and tell them about the orbs that just appeared. Some say that transparent spheres represent a soul reaching out to explain that something significant had happened and that the soul needs support, e.g. prayers to move on.

My wife sees the clearer orbs much more often, but it's a sign of sheer beauty when I witness one. I watched in awe as the bright clear globe danced around the bedroom before manoeuvring towards the top left-hand corner then shifting gracefully across the room. It disappeared but suddenly re-emerging outside the window, putting on a little show.

We often see green coloured orbs with the naked eye both in Cara's room and around the house and garden. Sometimes, coloured orbs will dance around Finn's head while playing. So, we use our feelings and gut instinct to make sense of these orbs based on the context of their appearance.

We awoke early that morning and were ready to face the day and give Cara the send-off that she deserved. We were also deeply saddened that she had departed. The angst and foreboding were palpable as the minutes ticked towards Cara's arrival by hearse (a long black vehicle used to carry Cara's small white coffin) from the funeral directors.

The house gradually filled with family and friends, including my Aunt and Uncle Mena and Ray, who travelled up from London. Faye's family arrived to wish everyone well before travelling onto the church. The funeral director kindly walked in front of the hearse for part of the journey.

It was later revealed that the funeral director's (Karen) husband (hearse driver) had recently been diagnosed with throat cancer. Regardless, he was determined to oversee the funeral after hearing about Cara's death.

Faye and I sat in the front seats of the second funeral car. Cara's beautiful picture smiled back at us from the base-end of the coffin in the leading car as we made the poignant short journey to the small Catholic church on Otley Old Road. My family and friends then helped me to carry Magoo down the aisle.

The mass itself was beautiful, and we found the strength from somewhere to complete the speeches, as Father Emmanuel had advised.

During the celebration of her life, we noticed how a flicker of light frequently appeared on the wall behind the pulpit. Maybe Cara was directing our attention away from the pain and onto something else?

Our friends Brian and Nicki flew in from Belfast, and Brian's brother Kevin travelled on the overnight bus from Glasgow to attend. He praised us for having the strength to speak and suggested that he couldn't have done it after losing a child. Kevin's an accomplished actor, so we appreciated the compliment.

To be honest, I was broken inside and felt like collapsing. The worst part was carrying Cara's little white coffin back through the church with support from friends and family including Gerry, Damien, Ray, and my friend Dee.

Cara's Obituary

"Words can't begin to express how proud and delighted we are to have had Cara for almost 12 years. Her 12th birthday would have been February 12th, 2020, and we are deeply saddened to be standing here on Cara's final day. She's been fortunate to have a great family on both sides of the Irish sea, through her grandparents David and Hazel, auntie Lucy and the girls and their extended families across Yorkshire and Italy.

And through her Irish grandparents Paddy and Marie, Sarah & Gerry, Lisa and Albert, Damien and Jacqui, Donna and Damo, Carla, and cousins. The messages, flowers, cards etc. From extended family and friends across the island of Ireland through to the USA, Tanzania, Canada and beyond illustrate the immense love and support for our precious Cara (or wee Magoo as we often called her).

Cara's life was hectic from day 1 when she was born 11 weeks early in 2008. She battled through various operations and stints in intensive care units and packed understaffed hospital wards. Mr Crabbe reversed Cara's Tracheostomy in 2012, and that was a real cause for celebration".

We took Cara to Majorca with the Tracheostomy and the look on her face as she played in the sea for the first time was priceless. She loved swimming and cycling in the Otley chevins with her brother and had a penchant for boxing.

Cara often woke me with a jab from her bright pink boxing gloves. For such a gentle soul, she was tough as old boots and enjoyed ganging up on me with her brother. She loved ballet and Irish dancing (looked more Morris dancing) as a kid. Still, she was hooked on Tiktok videos as she got older, with some of the funniest videos made with her little sidekick Finn and cousins Keira and Erika.

Cara absolutely loved her food. She was really into her curries in Leeds and Bradford, would often be seen in Leeds Market enjoying prawns and oysters [at Haye's seafood stall], and had a sweet tooth. She never liked a particular Thai restaurant in Leeds (even though she secretly loved the food), simply because there was no Wi-Fi.

I just found Cara's stash of chocolates hidden in my office, and we found the missing box of Quality Street in her room on boxing day with just empty wrappers. I was wondering why they were so quiet upstairs; her and her friends George, Emelia and brother Finn polished them all off. Her only problem was knowing when to say 'no' to food as she loved the food so much. Cara loved animals and always wanted a dog but couldn't because of her airway problems and allergies, which was a real shame.

Cara's caring and humane side were lovely for a child of that age. She was compassionate and often reached into her own pocket to help the homeless or pass on a sandwich or chocolate bar as we strolled through town. She cared for the poor and espoused the values of Holy Name primary school and Cardinal Heenan. A champion for human rights, we were proud to observe Cara's caring side and may her good friends in Year 7, and brother Finn continue that path.

We'd like to thank the staff at Copper Beech nursery ...through to Bramley St Peters school staff who were very helpful too during the Tracheostomy years. Cara was also blessed to have great teachers and peers at primary school and high school. Mrs Pearson, Mrs Harrington, Mr Greenfield [who called her Tinkerbell], Mr Hughes, Miss Given, and many others, including Sheila and the office team who were very accommodating to our family.

Cara was a beautiful young lady who was also very, very funny, and articulate. She had a real drawl Yorkshire sense of humour, and I, of course, was often in the firing line. She would often ask me about being a child in Belfast during the conflict as a bedtime story. When she was eight or nine, she asked me about life when I was eight or nine, same for 10 and more recently 11. When I kissed her goodnight, she often remarked – 'well that's brilliant, da. Thanks - another nice nightmare for me tonight' ??.

After spending hundreds of pounds on pebbles and many back-breaking hours doing the front garden, she came to the door and said to Faye and me, 'well, is that it? What's the big deal? I wouldn't have bothered' haha. Often when I got my hair cut, she would say, "...sure you don't have any hair, so what's the point" haha. Or she would describe my trips to the barbers as 'are you off for another gangster granny cut'.

She was always first into the front seat of her grandad's jeep & on our frequent trips to Ireland, my mate Dee McGahey would collect us from the airport. But Cara would be straight into the front passenger seat as Faye and I were ushered into the back. I hadn't a say in the matter. When Cara felt comfortable with people, she would be in her element.

Cara often said her prayers in Irish Gaelic (as my mother says, is the only language that the devil doesn't understand). In recent days, after praying for Cara, we (my wife, Finn, and me) have witnessed some truly amazing things around the house which would startle most people. Still, it assures us that Cara is at peace. Her energy and spirit are truly all around us. Kids, if you pray for Cara, you might just see something beautiful too.

Cara was excelling at the Spanish language and was doing well at school. She had a great group of friends, especially Sarah-Jane and Philip, who she cared for so much. And Alicia, who kindly brought Finn a present when she heard the news.

A typical Saturday morning at home was Cara and her partner in crime Finn, strolling downstairs. Bright lights on, curtains closed, cereal all over the worktop and kitchen floor, tv blaring on volume 50+ and not a care in the world - a trail of destruction every weekend without fail.

She was also a brilliant declutterer, and I was often bargaining her down to a few quid to tidy my office, which she was so accomplished at doing. She loved shopping, especially with her Granny Marie and her mum, and Claire's accessories was a firm favourite.

One time when shopping with her mum, in Claire's, she had her hair in a high ponytail. After leaving the store, Cara looked at her mum, in shock as she realised that a 12 pack of earrings got somehow stuck on her ponytail. So, she did the good deed and returned the earrings, but every time we passed Claire's in Trinity Centre, Cara would swing her ponytail and joke about 'what should we get this time'.

A lot of caring took place behind the scenes to manage her various health issues, but we'd do the same in a heartbeat just to have her home with us. We were so proud to call her our amazing daughter. She helped to make Finn the bright and articulate little character that he is today. Finn will miss his cuddles, fashion advice (for under fives haha), sleepovers, dance videos and swims with Cara in Majorca's coves. She left a massive void in our lives when Jesus decided to lift her from further misery and pending treatments or surgery.

We thank God for giving us these precious years, and the fantastic NHS for doing their best under such challenging circumstances. So, as I close this today, we can't help thinking of our beautiful Yorkshire Irish daughter who had a unique and delightful personality, but who was too kind and gentle for this world.

She wore battle scars from head, throat, and chest from previous surgery. Still, she always found a way to make us laugh through her quirky sense of humour, beautiful angelic voice, and her mums' lovely smile. Another angel has arrived in heaven, and may God hold her tightly in his arms until we meet again. Mary Queen of the Gael, pray for Cara.

Pauline's After The Funeral

Just before the hearse left the church for the cremation service, I considered singing a song to Cara in the cold and wet churchyard, but something held me back. Maybe it was Cara not wanting me to embarrass her one last time. So, we returned to the back of the church and passed on our thanks to everyone for attending.

We then travelled to Pauline's pub in Horsforth who kindly placed Cara's pictures around the large bar area and side rooms. Pauline played some Irish music in the background as she and her husband Steve ensured everyone was well fed.

It was great that Cara's school friends from High School took the day off school to show their respects. They arrived in hooded grey tops with signatures of class names from their last day of primary school in memory of Cara.

Pauline's was a regular spot when Faye's family met for lunch, and when my own family visited from Ireland. She and her husband and kids Andy and Amy were always so welcoming, and Cara loved to visit. She was often getting coins stuck in the games machine, and Pauline would be back and forth, laughing and joking with her.

After Pauline's, we met at our local Bangladeshi restaurant for a private family meal. The staff called me over, wondering why we were all in black and were stunned to hear about Cara. We would often sit as a family of four at the small table by the window.

They were saddened at the news but were curious about the paranormal and supernatural experiences at our home and mentioned that in their faith, a child is an angel – no matter what religion and that they would pray for her.

Cara's teachers and headmaster from High School (Mrs Powell-Wiffen and Mr Kelly) called by and supported us, before and after the funeral. Cara attended the school for one term but was made to feel very welcome. A book of remembrance was set up, and an annual mass is planned to be said in Cara's memory on her birthday.

The Room Is Buzzing

I was starkly awoken by something unexplainable, early one February morning. The energy was incredible, and the noise initially convinced me that the morning news presenters might be discussing an event such as an earthquake or a supersonic boom.

The whole bed continued to shake as if someone was forcibly jumping up and down. By now, I was fully awake and knew in my bones that it was Cara. I slipped under the duvet, shivering with disbelief, and trying to make sense of it all while Faye and Finn slept soundly next to me.

These types of events continued. For instance, two nights later, I awoke in the early hours of another cold February morning realising the brutal reality of Cara's loss. After praying for some peace of mind, I had a sixth sense that once again, something unexplainable was happening.

We've all experienced moments of "knowing" that defy logic and reason. But just what is this extra sense, and how does it work? Why do certain life experiences—falling in love, feeling intense grief, having a near-death experience— seem to bring it on? (21) (Naparstek, 2009).

Sensing intense energy, I peered left and immediately noticed two ultra-bright lights in a strange pattern: one to my left and the second which had enveloped Finn. Faye slept soundly to the far left. The light drew me to the pulsating appearance of a young Cara sat behind Finn, hugging him lovingly. Laying immediately to the left of me was a woman – elongated, but staring upwards, not making eye contact.

Being fully conscious of this beautiful and spiritual experience, I sat up on the corner of the bed and observed in awe for what seemed like a few minutes. I then quietly called Faye, who lifted her head from a deep sleep and looked at the figure behind Finn, saying ' Oh My God – look at the beautiful wings, and blue sparkles' then dozed back to sleep. I looked again to my left, and the angelic figure was gone, so too was the figure of Cara.

Climbing back into bed, I remember feeling immense calmness and strength before closing my eyes and digesting this profoundly spiritual experience.

Early the next morning, we discussed the visit: how the clear light reflected magnificently and how they radiated a pulsating glow, as clear as snow. Tiredness and lack of appetite were taking its toll on us both, but I was so relieved the next morning when Faye confirmed the experience and described the dazzle dust.

Our website created in memory of Cara (www.ismisecara.com) illustrates the different ways that the visitors present themselves at and around our home, including through a perceived human form. We find it satisfying to know that Cara's own Guardian Angel may have played a physically and spiritually protective role throughout her life.

Perhaps it explains why she survived for over 11 years when we could have lost her at 29 weeks (born 11 weeks early). We now believe that angels play a central role in helping people to navigate through the quagmire of life, intervening to avoid harmful situations.

They may appear in different guises. Still, we have never experienced anything like this before and feel so blessed to be chosen and visited. Blue sparkles also appeared when my sister read one of Lorna Byrne's books the previous evening in February 2020.

Carla: Kieran: the blue sparkles were all over that book last night when I was reading it. Definitely, our Cara is watching over us. The tall woman is probably your angel.

Carla: Lorna's book will definitely open your eyes and you will understand the orbs and sparkles. It's amazing; I was up until 2 am reading it.

On another night, I awoke from a peculiar dream. This time, it was to the pungent smell of smoke, like burning tyres. Jumping up, I followed my nose to what seemed like a potential fire downstairs.

But after checking, it quickly dawned that the smell wasn't real. Finn and Faye, we're asleep in bed as I went to the bathroom.

Returning to bed, I noticed a figure snuggled in between them. I knew in a heartbeat that it was Cara, as a young child – maybe three or four-years-old. Back turned, she faced her mum who was also facing the opposite way, sandwiched between Finn who lay on his back, higher up the pillow.

It is difficult to explain the feeling at seeing our beautiful little girl at peace on the bed, with her fuzzy dark brown hair and what appeared to be a frilly dress.

My heart was racing, but for some reason, I grew concerned for Finn. So, I reached out and was relieved to feel his warm breath on the back of my hand. I then paused momentarily, just silently observing, before climbing into bed and saying a brief prayer, feeling overwhelmed but not frightened.

Turning again to my left-hand side, I noticed how the figure had disappeared and was replaced by a more substantial sized figure which was snug close to Finn's immediate left-hand side, again with back turned.

Through a gap in the curtains, the moonlight reflected what seemed like a pink coloured pyjama top. Presuming it was Faye, I reached across and stroked her warm back. After laying on my back again, I arose to find an empty space, and Faye some feet away wearing her blue and white pyjama top. The figures had disappeared, so I prayed a second time before drifting off to sleep in a state of peace.

The next morning, Faye, mentioned how she had prayed and asked Cara to protect Finn, who was nervous and afraid to sleep on his own.

This conscious experience seemed to have coincided with another of my sister Carla's unconscious dreams from the night before. She vividly described how a young Cara visited our home in Belfast in the company of another child while her 'mum was in the hospital'.

Donegal Plaque

Later in February 2020, we decided to visit a pizza restaurant on Kirkstall Road, Leeds for the first time since Cara passed. It was one of Cara's most popular restaurants but felt empty there without her.

As we reminisced about the good times, I sent pictures of Faye and Finn to my family, who quickly replied about the ghostly appearance of faces peering back through the window. It was a quiet, frosty evening, and no one was near the window when the pictures were taken directly opposite our seats. As we ate, a flurry of WhatsApp messages arrived from the South of Ireland.

My sister and brother headed back to Donegal for a special visit to remember Cara along with their partners and kids. After time relaxing in Ardara, they stopped for prayers at the beautiful discrete waterfall Assarenca Eas (22).

Damien's friend Barry crafted a stunning plaque of Cara with a Yorkshire Rose and Celtic cross, which they attached to a large stone at the base of the site.

Our friends Maura and Brenda and their kids stopped at the plaque the next day for prayers before driving back to Belfast; Cara would have loved that. Donegal is an extraordinarily beautiful county. Cara and Finn were fascinated to hear about the fairy houses scattered around the waterfall area.

At the pizza restaurant, we continued to view the stream of images from the plaque laying ceremony at Assarenca Eas. The spirits seemed to have joined them on their big adventure. The waterfall, rocks and bramble seemed to have been transformed into faces of souls and angel-like figures.

The plaque itself had appeared to transform into a God-like figure at an altar with angels kneeling beneath (See Exhibit C on www.ismisecara.com). My mother described it as akin to an apparition. It was increasingly apparent that something magical was happening, everywhere and anywhere.

Ashes And The Emerald Angel

We visited Karen at the funeral home in Horsforth, Leeds to collect Cara's ashes. Slaters were terrific from day one, especially Lisa, Karen, and Beverley who went-over-and-above to make the funeral unique and special.

After the funeral, we went to collect the ashes and met with Beverley –who explained how when her husband passed, someone called at their home to purchase his guitar. As he drove away, she looked out the window, and it was her husband's date of birth on his registration plate.

Beverly believed it was a sign of devotion from her deceased husband. On her first, solo holiday abroad to Tenerife, she entered the hotel foyer, and was amazed to hear an old and obscure song loved by her husband.

She then hugged us before we climbed into the car, with the ashes placed on Faye's knee in the front seat. As we drove home, Cara's favourite song began to play on the radio.

Weeks earlier, we asked Sarah-Jane to pick Cara's songs for the funeral party at 'Donegal Pauline's'. Everything seemed so connected and surreal as we drove home in harmony with Magoo.

That night after lighting a candle next to Cara's ashes, we prayed and discussed her short and beautiful life. Faye noticed the candle glowing before the flame gradually rose and merged into an emerald green figure. Within seconds, a shimmering angel-like image with poised magenta coloured wings, small dainty head and long body eventually became separated from the flame. Rising majestically, it then started to float along the wall.

Shortly afterwards, I phoned my sister Donna to explain what had just happened. As we spoke, I described to Donna how at that very moment, a row of spinning green orbs hovered and stared me in the face. Within a minute or so, one slowly twirled towards the far side of the kitchen. By now, Donna was getting real-time commentary as I explained how the orb was growing and spinning before my very eyes until it reached the size of a human head.

Situated approximately eight foot off the floor, directly above the wine rack, it slowly turned around and faced me. I called Faye into the kitchen, but she could only observe the small green orbs, not the large orb in the corner.

Amidst the excitement and disbelief, I slowly informed Donna about how beautiful its hair was, but it took a few seconds before it revealed its human-like features. I nearly fainted once I recognised Cara's distinctive eyes, nose, and lips. It wasn't explicitly human, more a blend of physical and mint green smoulder. Initially feeling emotional and overwhelmed, I watched in awe as the spirits disappeared into thin air, and my mood changed to one of intense happiness at seeing something magical unfold in real-time.

Taking Ashes to Belfast

We travelled from Manchester airport to Belfast, carting Cara's ashes in a small wooden box. It was sad to experience that airport again, having been there previously in happier times. After delivering the ashes to my mums' home, we gathered around the table and prayed. Her little cousins were devastated and cried uncontrollably during the prayers.

We then ordered Chinese food and spent some quality time together. It was an opportunity to discuss the loss but also explain how fortunate Cara was to avoid chemo and radiation. Cara was such a pure child but a constant worrier that it would have been terrifying to see her suffer or to witness her demise.

We booked a hotel room in Belfast city centre and headed back there at around 10pm. I twisted and turned and by 4am, was still awake, feeling burnt out and overwhelmed with grief. Looking to the side, the large picture on the wall seemed distorted. It made me feel uneasy, as I blinked and refocused trying to figure out its meaning. It appeared like a distorted image of a girl, with a device protruding from her brain.

When Faye awoke, she agreed that it was a bizarre-looking artsy picture, and quite disturbing. Faye then pointed to a green orb flying overhead, above our bed. The room was compact, so it didn't take long for me to notice this small but beautiful green figure with little white wings manoeuvre around the room. We just sat and watched in awe.

While brushing my teeth, I noticed how the steam from the shower had transformed the shower door into almost a biblical type image. It was akin to a collection of spirits and souls. Faye and I viewed and discussed the visitors before taking pictures and sharing with my family.

That night crammed into my mum's kitchen; our whole family had an incredible experience. Orbs of different shapes and sizes appeared. Approximately 15 of us watched what seemed like a firework show. Cara seemed to be showing us that her soul was far from dead; it was alive and kicking.

Child: Belfast Airport

We bid farewell to the family before my brother Damien drove us to the airport. On route, we stopped to collect little Emmet before venturing onwards through the icy backroads of Hannahstown, towards Belfast International Airport.

Flicking through the pictures of orbs and souls on my smartphone, I noticed how specific family pictures had somehow changed into religious-like figures and other souls. I wasn't looking forward to the flight, after another light sleep and was feeling down about leaving Ireland.

As we approached the gates, the security lady came and offered to 'help you to get the children through'. She then said, 'Let's get the children in the middle' while offering to scan the tickets. We then presented her with the e-tickets via the airline app.

The security lady walked behind us while simultaneously looking at her mobile device. Looking bemused, she asked, 'Where's the other child?' to which she then remarked 'Sorry, my eyes must be playing tricks on me'.

I didn't have to look at Faye to know what she was thinking. It was a mixture of bewilderment and amazement - a feeling that Cara was with us on our journey to Ireland and back to Leeds.

As we left, we noticed how the lady stared through us, looking convinced. We regret not returning to ask what she had seen, but have a pretty good idea.

153

Our flight navigated through a rocky storm that had just hit Ireland and Britain. We decided to avoid the train to Leeds and stay overnight at the same hotel chain in Manchester.

An older member of staff with a white beard offered to help carry the bags to our room. There was something curious about him, and when inside the room, I asked why the hotel would use that very picture because it looked dismal. But he said that the artist wouldn't care what I thought, because his work was so successful.

Later, while unpacking, I stared at the same picture in that hotel room – a case of 'painting by numbers'. We were already a bit spooked about the Belfast visits, the orbs and especially the angelic figure in mint green floating around the Belfast hotel room. Now, this picture in Manchester was back on our minds.

It was unreal to see even more images appear. Again, after showering, the steam on the shower door gradually resembled something from the bible – a mixture of remarkable characters and lost souls.

It was so reassuring to know that Faye and Finn were witnessing the same things, otherwise, I'd be starting to question my sanity. It was also reassuring that family and friends confirmed that they too could see these images in the frequent WhatsApp videos and pictures.

We believe that one regular visitor was Padre Pio. So many times, Padre Pio seemed to appear in the images. I remember saying the Novena Online for Cara through the Clonard Monastery website and decided to take a picture of the altar. Such a beautiful church with a significant history. It was a base for discussions that led to the Irish peace process agreement. Later that night, when checking my phone, my heart skipped a beat as the image of an older man appeared, with a beam of light shining from his mouth – amongst other faces. Another visual experience was of a girl in our living room with a bearded man, kneeling (See Exhibit D www.ismisecara.com).

Chapter 3 ~ Sense Making

Cara's all around?

Peculiar things continued to occur in different locations, which often startled us when we weren't expecting it. Finn slept in his bed for the first time since Cara's passing, while Faye and I sat downstairs watching television.

We felt relieved that he had dozed off in his bed without any tears. An hour or so later, we heard a commotion, so I nipped up to his bedroom to check.

Finn was standing at the end of his bed in the darkened room. He wasn't crying, just standing, pointing to the ceiling, and staring upwards - observing something or someone in a trance-like state with his eyes opened.

Maybe it was Cara, or perhaps a Guardian Angel? Lifting him off his feet, I carried him back to bed, tucked him in and off he went.

Apparently, our deceased loved ones are incredibly creative and relentless when they wish to communicate. 'Visitors' may often include family, friends and 'unemployed angels' as Lorna Byrne describes them.

They use different methods to transmit messages and are innovative and resourceful – whether it's through images on curtains (See Exhibit E and Exhibit E* on www.ismisecara.com), figures appearing through rays of sunlight or different sized orbs spinning around the home (See Exhibit F; F*&F** on www.ismisecara.com).

One day, on our daily lockdown walk, Finn slipped off his bike onto a wet concrete kerb. He was up in seconds with a small scratch. We then decided to take a short cut through the woods close to our home in Horsforth.

As we approached a large tree, the face of a man– a holy type figure seemed to be etched into the bark. Always conscious that my mind could be playing tricks, I checked again, and the face was clearly peering back at me.

This type of event happens to us quite often. For instance, something strange happened in real-time as I spoke to my mother - a deeply religious woman, a few nights before Finn's 5th birthday. A picture of Mohammed Ali downing Sonny Liston, which hangs on my study wall, became populated with faces.

The images resembled a mixture of human and alien types. All of this initially made us believe that Cara was using her energy to reach out to us. Maybe Cara was playing a role in transporting lost souls to the physical world in their quest for prayers? But Lorna Byrne (a world renowned spiritual teacher, international bestselling author and philanthropist from Ireland) explained otherwise when we discussed this with her in October 2020.

Finn initially struggled to cope after Cara's loss. They were so alike with a beautiful brother-sister bond. He often asks if Cara will return and believes that Cara has returned to heaven in the form of a baby.

Finn also asks if-and-when we can also turn into babies and join her. We assure Finn that we will all be together again. He finds that quite comforting and soothing.

We often see inexplicable flashes or orbs in the garden. The sunlight seems to dip and shine onto Finn more-so than others (See Exhibit G and Exhibit G* on www.ismisecara.com).

We are aware of the potential for bias or misinterpretation, but both see things with our own eyes before capturing through the lens of different smartphones and cameras. Sometimes we think that maybe his big sister is in a powerful realm and looking after him.

Coroners Letter

Official confirmation came through from the Coroner's Office. We then registered Cara's death after telephone conversations with the Coroner, his secretary and other agencies including the child bereavement team.

An eventful and distressing few days in April 2020 followed for us as we relived the events of that fateful night. The memories came flooding back. It was further confirmation that Cara was indeed gone from the physical world. Darkness descended the house after encountering more of her clothes and personal belongings.

A series of events happened after an uneasy weekend, trying to cope with the physical loss while maintaining social distancing measures and hanging around the house. One night in April, Faye was exhausted and went to bed early. Later, after a quick prayer in Cara's room, I climbed into bed as Faye murmured something which I couldn't comprehend.

First thing next morning, she described a spiritual appearance through the wardrobe mirror. Before drifting off, a face that strongly resembled Padre Pio appeared in the glass mirror. The floating image slowly changed to a girl's face and then disappeared. We prayed to Padre Pio to protect Cara every night of her life.

161

Before sleeping, Cara would kiss the cover of a Padre Pio memorial card dedicated to my cousin Constantine and his father Costello who died in recent years.

Amidst the grief and the pain of Cara's loss, were glimpses of light from our experiences with the spirit world. Prayers gave us the strength to cope, and one night before sleeping, I asked my Guardian Angel what their name was.

Later, the word 'CORNELIUS' reverberated loud and clear. Next morning on a long walk around Horsforth, I Googled the name Cornelius and was amazed to read that it was a fourth-century Saint.

More recently, I searched to find the translation of the word in Irish Gaelic and was amazed to find the name 'Conn' or 'Constantine'.

My cousin Constantine died after a long battle with leukaemia. Cara often prayed for his health and afterwards, for his soul: 'The salvation of Cornelius and his household marks a critical turning point in the early church's commission to take the gospel "to the ends of the earth" as Jesus had instructed' (Acts 1:8).

During a previous set of pictures capturing the flying orbs in Cara's room in February 2020, we noticed what appeared to be a white feather laid across an image of Padre Pio's picture (See Exhibit H on www.ismisecara.com).

Cara's bedroom continues to be a hive of vibrancy and energy, and that night was no different. We believe that these experiences are related to Cara and that she is somehow trying to ease the heartache of our loss.

For instance, we wrote the early sections of this book from our back garden in Leeds, and at one stage, were surrounded by white feathers.

Early on Easter Sunday morning, 2020, we noticed that a beautiful wood pigeon lay dead beneath the garden patio table.

We disposed of the bird, but scores of exquisite white feathers remained on the grass for many weeks afterwards (See Exhibit I on www.ismisecara.com).

One possibility is that it hit the back window close to Cara's favourite seat, and a magpie may have plucked it? But there was no blood on the bird or marks on the window, just a mass of feathers.

Maybe Cara was reaching out and sharing her love and affection? The pain of Cara's loss is often quelled by some phenomenon or other which pops up and distracts us, just like the flickers or the orbs, and takes us into a more positive space.

The little things hurt the most, and we still haven't found the strength to unpack her school bag or exercise bag. Her bedroom remains a place of tranquillity and peace.

It is, without doubt, a fountain of energy. Although, it still destroys us to think about events that fateful night and the horrors of finding our little girl's chilled and lifeless body.

Vision Of Child And Girl

A different pattern of dreams and conscious visitations followed over the following days, which continued to comfort rather than distress us.

We continued to see things in real-time with the naked eye but were also having the most vivid and spiritual dreams. Finn's a restless sleeper, so I use a pillow to convert part of our King-sized bed into an almost single compartment to try for a better night's sleep.

One early morning as the light was shining through the blinds, I looked to the right-hand side towards the glass mirror and noticed what appeared to be the arms of a baby.

Looking further into the mirror, I observed a little child's face peering back at me; eyes wide open but appearing serene. Feeling totally at peace, I rolled around again and checked on Finn and Faye.

Both were asleep, and then I looked at the tiny child – face-to-face for a few moments before laying back down, feeling strangely contented but bemused.

I closed my eyes, trying to make sense of it all and started to say the rosary as I have done most days since Cara passed. After dozing off for a short while, I was startled by something and turning around; noticed that the baby figure had disappeared.

165

Laying back for a few seconds, I turned to my left again and witnessed a tall girl with long dark hair sitting on the side of the bed. Very tall, like a large but not obese person. I reached across and felt her back before laying back.

Something prompted me to bounce up again and glancing left, Faye and Finn were facing each other and still asleep. The girl had gone. Feeling overwhelmed, I remember feeling fascinated and puzzled, knowing for sure that Cara was nearby. But what did it mean? I couldn't wait to tell Faye about the visit when she woke.

Girl With The Long Dark Hair

On Sunday 19.4.2020, Faye lay restless in bed thinking about Cara and struggled to sleep. Turning and stretching out her hand, she touched what she felt was the back of Finn's head. After a few moments, Faye noticed how plush and soft the hair felt. Her hand continued past the point where Finn's short hair should have stopped, travelling past the neck before resting on the lower back area. Recognising the dark hair, she immediately sensed the close and immediate presence of Cara.

Faye described how she then drifted off to sleep and dreamt that Cara was standing at the bedroom door – a full-sized appearance in her pink and grey leopard-print pyjamas. Running forward towards the bathroom or Finn's bedroom, she reappeared again at the bedroom doorway.

Just then, as Faye and I (this time in the dream) remarked to each other, 'Was that Cara at the door?', she turned towards us both with the biggest and most beautiful smile before slowly fading. Faye described a feeling of contentment, reassured that Cara was at peace. I sensed peace, too, when told of the physical, conscious and unconscious experiences afterwards.

The unconscious (dream) and conscious (seeing and feeling in real-time) are inextricably connected and must be happening for a reason.

Early January, when my family visited us in Leeds after Cara died, one of Finn's toy cars flew off the top of the microwave and across the kitchen floor. My mother was shocked because no one could have thrown it.

I then placed it back on the microwave and put a small box in front just in case it had somehow slipped off, and we continued to talk. A few minutes later, it was as if someone had lifted the car and flung it across the room again. Not in a negative way, but more playful – which made us think that Cara was up to her mischief.

That night, my sisters were resting downstairs on our sofa when they observed the coloured orbs flying around the darkened living room.

The God Spot

Finn turned five years old on 30.4.2020, and it was his first birthday without Cara. I passed my driving test on April 30th, 2008, which was also Cara's initial due date. Early that morning, Finn tried to jump on my back as I walked around our bed. After telling him off in case he injured himself, I mumbled something along the lines of 'you can't jump that far anyway, it's impossible', but then explained to him that somebody could also interpret it as 'I'm Possible', and never to give up.

I often said this to Cara when she was feeling low. When we awoke on May 1st, 2020, Faye mentioned a dream about the numbers 19:26 and asked me to check it online. We were surprised to see words from the bible:

'Matthew 19:26 King James Version (KJV). But Jesus beheld them, and said unto them, with men, this is impossible; but with God, all things are possible' (23).

Cara's brainstem tumour opened our eyes to the brutal reality of this disease. I remember seeing Cara in anguish after her release from the hospital after the biopsy. Tiny samples of the tumour left a slight wobble in her eye. Her balance was off, and she looked to us, in peril.

As we sat on her bed, she asked me my age and when I said '44', she paused and said: 'well you've only about 50 years left'. I joked that 'I'd be delighted to live until 94'.

Looking concerned, I asked her if everything was OK. She then told me about a dream where she had died during surgery and how she observed us both walking down the hospital corridor.

An acute episode had indeed occurred during the biopsy. Thankfully, she was saved by the superb skill and care from John and the neuro team. Maybe she had a glimpse into the afterlife?

Some nights later, as we tucked Cara into bed, she shared another dream, this time about a little pink coffin. We often dreaded walking Cara to the theatre before an operation.

Afterwards, she would often ask why the medical team told such bad jokes – 'as if surgery was a joke' itself. She could not see the method in their madness.

Sitting or lying together on her bed at home, we often focused on the wind chimes above our heads and feeling a sense of dread that her time might come sooner than we think.

The brainstem is such a sensitive zone, and just a few millimetres of tumour growth can have catastrophic consequences.

Cara's initial biopsy in September 2018 left a scar behind and above her right ear which took months to heal. She would often jump or groan when skin stretched around the wound.

In 2008, a psychologist at the University of Missouri called Brick Johnstone undertook a sensitive study into patients with traumatic brain injuries around the right parietal lobe – the part of the brain located slightly above the right ear. Johnstone, Bodling et al. (2012) found that patients with damage to their right parietal lobe (the bit on the side of your head above your ear) report being more spiritual than patients with impairment in other areas (24).

Their follow-up study explored 20 patients with traumatic brain injury in different parts of the brain. Johnstone and colleagues found that patients with damage to their right parietal lobe (measured by their ability to judge the orientation of lines and ability to identify the fingers on their left hand) were more spiritual.

They also tended to score higher on measures of forgiveness (so they were less 'self-oriented') as well on measures of spiritual transcendence (tending to agree with statements like 'I feel the presence of a higher power').

In contrast, patients with damage to their frontal lobe (measured using a kind of 'connect the letters and numbers' puzzle) tended to be less likely to engage in religious practices (25). Explorations into the neural spot - a religious or 'God Spot' show that it may inadvertently control religious belief across a spectrum from apathy and light association with religion through to fundamentalism (Christian, Islamic or beyond).

There may even be 'God Spots' showing different regions of the brain as the premise (biological) of religious belief. Johnstone and Cohen (2019) continued their exploration into neuroscience and religion by taking an interdisciplinary approach to explain the science of transcendence (26).

We also find it fascinating how the intelligent mind tends to heat-seek, adapt, and transform itself to enhance its chances of survival and sustainability.

Reaching Out To Lorna Byrne

Our family in Ireland suggested that we reach out to Lorna Byrne for advice on the supernatural and paranormal experiences in Leeds, Manchester and Ireland since Cara died. Email correspondence was made with Lorna's team between February and April 2020. Gradually feeling overwhelmed (see images under Exhibit J on www.ismisecara.com), we needed answers from someone connected to the spirit world (not a clairvoyant). An excerpt from our initial email to Lorna's team is below:

'Hello Lorna: Since our 11-year-old daughter Cara died on 29.12.2019, many amazing events have happened at our home in Leeds and with family in Ireland. These include:

- Frequent sights of beautiful coloured Orbs after praying;
- Family pictures changing to faces of deceased people;
- Bathroom tiles changing to people's faces;
- White feathers appearing on Padre Pio's picture;
- Orbs following family around their homes in Ireland;
- Visions of Angels floating through the house;
- the sight of Angel like figures on our bed, glowing white.

And many other events and experiences. We don't feel afraid but wonder what messages are behind all of this. We would appreciate it if you could speak with us tomorrow (after or before) the Webinar?

Lorna Byrne's team invited Faye, Finn, and I to her Manchester 2020 event ('Lorna Byrne in Conversation' on behalf of The Lorna Byrne Children's Foundation event'). Lorna subsequently postponed the event due to the pandemic and kindly invited us to a follow-up Webinar instead.

The Lorna Byrne Children's Foundation (27) believes that all children have a right to be happy, healthy and safe. We support amazing initiatives to help marginalised and vulnerable children and young people in Ireland and around the world. We believe each and every one of us has a role to help the children of the world; they are our children and it's their future. From wellbeing and health to education, integration and humanitarian aid, our projects transform children's lives.

LORNA BYRNE
Children's Foundation

For more information on the Lorna Byrne Children's Foundation and to support the charity, please visit www.foundation.lornabyrne.com

We were relieved to participate in the follow-up Webinar. Lorna answered many questions from the public about angels, souls, and guides; yet we never spoke or communicated directly to Lorna during the event.

May 18th, 2020 began as an uneventful Monday morning in Leeds. Things quickly changed when Pearl, Lorna Byrne's daughter and manager, suggested a Skype meeting with Lorna on Wednesday, May 20th. Our first offer of a personal, private chat.

After lunch, we walked around Hawksworth Wood and back home through Horsforth to clear our heads. Finn agreed to walk the 5+ miles on the condition of ice cream on the way back. It was fun and games when he realised that the shop was closed.

Still, we identified some critical questions for Lorna, such as: 'Why Have These Visitors Only Appeared Since Cara Died?' 'What's Their Intention'? 'Are They Lost Souls Looking for Prayers?'.

Father Emmanuel gave us strength and hope that it was Cara's way of reaching out. Still, there was more to it, and we needed to reveal and decipher the hidden messages. After dinner, I decided to view some of the recent videos and images.

Faye then emerged to tell me about a hive of activity in Cara's room and how she asked Cara 'I take it that you or the angels have been talking to Lorna Byrne' before a brief flicker emerged.

Seconds later, it converged into what she described as a silent lightning strike, with sparks and streamers—just a beautiful and calming experience.

I immediately sensed Cara's energy after going to investigate. It was apparent that the faces had also changed on the curtains. These were different creatures, e.g. some medieval-looking, others perhaps holy, but we weren't sure (Exhibit K on www.ismisecara.com).

There was a mix of all sorts, including eerie, younger, and more ambiguous figures. We couldn't quite decipher if some were animals or humans because of the angle and light in the room.

Finn dozed off to sleep at about 8pm, and we sat on the sofa talking about Cara and the meeting before heading to bed around 10.30pm. Once the light went out, I snuggled in with Faye as she stared towards the ceiling in silence.

After a few minutes, she pointed upwards, saying 'look at the green orbs'. It took me about 30 seconds to focus before I saw the mint green figures amidst what seemed like black fog and grey patches. The small orbs flew across the room – up and down, and side to side.

For the next hour or so, we just lay back and observed this incredible display of energy that was hard to describe. Just an array of objects and shapes, floating around with coloured orbs occasionally piercing the darkness.

Strange things came floating as if crashing into us without physically touching. We remember seeing what seemed like an octopus shape in the dark, as the room buzzed with energy.

Faye drifted off as I lay, wondering why this was happening but feeling more confused than concerned. Our home is usually an abundance of positive energy, and having faith gives us strength. We assumed that Lorna may have communicated with her angel about Cara and felt more convinced that the visitors were there for a reason.

I soon dozed off and dreamt about an Archangel (type figure) who stood next to several boxes. The first few boxes were radiating light while several others remained unlit.

Then a young fella appears, driving madly in a car, trying to escape from someone. I awoke and drank some water before drifting back to sleep and straight back into the same dream, standing next to the holy figure and watching the boy being praised before two more of the boxes lit up in a fantastic glow – as if they were on fire but without flames.

Feeling uneasy, I woke up again and lay awake for a few minutes before turning towards Faye. By now Finn had climbed into the middle of our bed. Still, I noticed that something was glowing on Faye's pyjamas. I nearly jumped 10 feet when I saw another tiny baby, almost premature looking, was lying on Faye's belly staring at me.

Its head and neck were visible above the quilt. I sat up and silently observed for a few minutes, before laying back down, closing my eyes and silently praying. Finn tends to either laugh, tap my head, or gently nudge my back when I pray to Cara in silence.

I often mention to Faye that it seems like he is responding to something, e.g. Cara or something in the spirit world. By now, it was 4.30am, and I was worried about facing the day without much sleep, but I managed to doze off a third time shortly afterwards.

Now, I was in another deep dream, this time sitting in our living room in Beechmount, Belfast, with my father, Paddy. I remember saying, 'Da, look at the orbs' before he agreed that 'aye, I can see that'.

The small translucent orb spun about before stopping above our heads and expanding into the size of a hurling ball. First the eyes, then nose before the unmistakable smile of Cara appeared. It was smaller in size but like the physical visit in our kitchen in Leeds when talking to my sister Donna.

It was one of those perfect dreams—a bit like dreaming of Christmas when you are a kid. Reality kicked in as I opened my eyes and realised that these dreams are happening alongside the real-life and real-time events that we were observing.

Faye and I lay and discussed the remarkable events from the night before. We knew in our hearts that something surreal had taken place and believed that Cara was in a special place.

It was evident to us that Lorna's intervention and decision to meet with us had stimulated the spirit world in ways that we do not fully understand.

Lorna Delivers a Message From Cara

Lorna Byrne called at 10am, and we were so glad to meet with such a unique lady over Skype. She exuded love and kindness in abundance and immediately made us feel at ease.

After asking about our location, I then described Cara's history from premature birth and through the various health battles until her death.

After a few minutes, Lorna paused before telling us that she has been in touch with Cara and has a special message to share with us.

We were stunned as she explained how they have been communicating and how Cara wanted us to know that she loved every moment of life with us. Accepting that things were often difficult, but that Cara loves us all dearly. She wants us to be happy, and to live life to the full, especially for Finn.

I then explained the incredible experiences at our home since Pearl had confirmed the meeting. For instance, how a small baby was lying on Faye's stomach, snuggled in, the night before.

Lorna asked if Faye had ever had a miscarriage before explaining how that would be our baby, a little boy.

We both felt emotional and realised that the experiences around the house increasingly made more sense.

179

When I relayed the dream about the Archangel and golden boxes, Lorna was intrigued to know which Archangel. She asked 'Which was it? Michael? Gabriel'? I had a feeling that it was an Archangel without really knowing for sure.

The Catholic Church identifies with three Archangels mentioned in the Holy Scriptures: 'Michael ("Who is like God?"), Gabriel ("God's Power") and Raphael ("God's Doctor")' The Sacred Scripture then attributes a particular mission to each Archangel.

Michael is the warrior who fights against Satan and his emissaries (Jn 9, Ap 12, 7, cf. Zec 13: 1-2), the defender of those who love God (Dn 10, 13.21), the protector of the people of God (Dn. 12, 1);

Gabriel is one of the spirits closest to God, before his heavenly throne (Lk 1, 19), the one who revealed to Daniel the secrets of God's plan (Dn 8, 16; 9, 21-22), announced to Zechariah the birth of John the Baptist (Lk 1, 11-20) and to Mary that of Jesus (Lk 1, 26-38);

Raphael stands before the throne of God (Tb 12, 15, see Rev 8: 2), accompanied and protects Tobias in his perilous journey and healed his father from blindness and his future bride from the influence of evil. (28)

We continued to explain the various interventions and sights around the house and beyond. Lorna nodded in acknowledgement and explained how this was something that only happens to certain people.

And how people often have experienced phenomenon without realising their significance or meaning and are oblivious. She mentioned how, when a single white feather appears, it is usually a message of love from the angels and a sign of spiritual guidance.

Lorna stressed how God loved everyone, of every religion and creed. She also confirmed that my cousin Constantine, who had died recently, was now with Cara. I asked if the purity and age of Cara would place her in a different realm. Lorna explained how our souls are interconnected and how our families will be together again.

Lorna then heard Finn in the background and invited him to join the conversation. After asking his age, we discussed Cara's original birth date - April 30th, the date of Finn's birth, seven years later.

She then remarked how 'he was still very new from heaven'. Finn was stood in his Ireland shirt, smiling, and chatting with Lorna for a few minutes before running off to play. Lorna mentioned how we were both very spiritual people and that there were many messages behind our supernatural experiences.

During the meeting, the audio connection dropped, but Lorna remained visible in the video feed. We managed to finish the conversation shortly afterwards on a different device. My family wonder if she was liaising with her angels at that moment? Lorna then asked if there were any final questions.

Faye asked about the sightings at the airport, and how the security guard stepped out and asked about the second child. She believed that 'yes, that would have been your daughter Cara' and that she found from other families that their bereaved child would accompany them on journeys.

181

Lorna expressed Cara's desire for us to have fun and live life to the full. I asked if she could see our Guardian Angels in that same meeting, but she couldn't do so over a virtual connection and small screen. We also asked why Cara always looked so well, and why, even in her worst moments, looked radiant and healthy. So much so that Dr Phil Chetcuti (Respiratory Consultant) placed a letter on the hospital A&E patient information system. He advised that when Cara presents, 'she will look OK but often won't be. She must be thoroughly assessed'.

Lorna smiled and mentioned that '...this was because her soul was shining so brightly'. Faye then asked what age Cara would be in heaven, and she explained how the spirits of souls are ageless – that there were no space and time constraints and that she is often between heaven and earth, with us.

Faye also mentioned how her folks had placed Cara's ashes under the Willow tree and how little butterflies constantly fluttered around that area. And how a white feather given to her mum at the time of laying her ashes had gone missing. In a panic, her mum spent hours looking for it, pulling the place apart. Later, she saw her reflection in the mirror and there it was - stuck to her face.

Similar things have occurred at Cara's rose bush in my mum's garden containing ashes. A tiny butterfly seems to have made the bush its home. Lorna mentioned that the spirit of Cara will often blend into the figures of others and that we have probably already passed her in the street.

If we ever encounter someone who resembles Cara, or from a distance, think for a second that it could be Cara, to never approach or invade their space. They are straight from heaven, so pure, and on their spiritual journeys.

Lorna continued to explain how Cara 'absolutely adored both sets of grandparents and loved everyone in her family so much'. Lorna's eyes lit up again as she described Cara as much more than perfect and how 'it was almost indescribable how perfect she was'. Lorna then remarked how she wished that she could give us both a big hug. Lorna has a beautiful soul herself. It was such an extraordinary meeting with a very precious and amazing woman at a time of raw grief.

Minutes after the meeting, a delivery team arrived to drop off building materials, including soundproof boards, and it was hectic trying to get the materials through the patio doors. Faye's sister Lucy had an appointment at the breast clinic at the same time as Lorna's meeting (10am) to check a potential problem, (which we considered a strange coincidence). Still, luckily the news was good, and everyone in the family felt much more optimistic about the future.

We took Finn for a sandwich and walk on the Leeds and Liverpool canal in the fierce heat. It was 26 degrees Celsius, and as we returned to the car, I called my Aunt Mena to discuss Lorna's meeting. Mena also mentioned how one of the recent pictures that I had sent to her was very similar to an 18th-century figure wearing a cherub.

We often see a bizarre blend of medieval and biblical souls in traditional garments, often with dogs, horses, and other animals. Bizarrely, they often change in appearance and later return to their original form. But Lorna has offered us great hope and put our minds at rest. We now have something to cherish before it is our time to meet with Cara again.

183

Red Orbs Are Circling

Later than evening, Finn was restless and took a while to drift off. At 5am, we woke from a night of deep sleep to loud crashing noise as if a window had been smashed.

After checking, we noticed that our large bedroom picture had fallen. Bizarrely, the nail remained in the wall.

I then dozed off to sleep, and when I woke about 8am, Faye, described how a team of (over a dozen) small red orbs, had returned and circled the spot where the picture had fallen - about five foot from the floor.

These appeared at around 7am. She described it as akin to twinkling fairy lights as the orbs spread around the site of the picture. Maybe Cara was sending a message?

We have since replaced the old photo with a canvas showing Cara, Finn, Faye, and me praying at a statue of Our Lady in Ardara, Donegal. Red orbs are often associated with protection.

It was surreal that something could happen like this in a physical sense. Lorna's energy seems to have permeated into our home in a way that we cannot fully explain.

Things continued to confound us that day, with many quirky faces appearing in the most mundane places, which we continue to capture on camera.

Let The Healing Begin

My family often remind me of excerpts from Lorna Byrne's books when trying to make sense of it all - both Cara's death and the after events. But what exactly are these orbs?

Who are the visitors in the night? Why are there countless souls and maybe lost souls appearing in different guises?

One image seemed particularly haunting. My brother sent a picture of his son, Emmet, shortly after Cara passed. Compelled to look closer, we zoomed to the image of a figure who seemed like the devil himself.

My family largely agreed. Terry Boyle (RIP) wasn't so sure and remarked that: 'It's the last thing Satan would do. Otherwise, he'd terrify people and risk converting or returning folk to God'.

Terry made sense, and his intervention helped to lift a sense of unease that developed over that Friday evening.

We believe that the healing from Cara's loss is happening in God's own unique way, for as Lorna Byrne mentioned, He knows best.

I remember conversations with our good friends Tony and Gary Kelly now based in California about life after their parents passed.

Tony described his mother's (Lily's) death as if someone has plucked colours from the rainbow. Lily often prayed for Cara, and we treasure her lovely cards and letters during the tough times. She never mentioned her own health problems and was only interested in Cara's wellbeing.

When I lived in the United States, Gary would often play The Furey's song 'The Old Man'. He would discuss the lyrics in the context of his father, John, who was in his later years and wondered how long he'd have left. John was a gentleman, a proper countryman, and I still associate the song with him.

The Tears Have All Been Shed Now.
We've Said Our Last Goodbyes.
His Soul's Been Blessed.
And He's Laid to Rest.
It's Now I Feel Alone.
He Was More Than Just a Father.
A Teacher, My Best Friend.
He Can Still Be Heard.
In the Tunes We Shared
When I Play Them on My Own

Excerpts from The Fureys – My Old Man (29)

Lorna also mentioned to us that healing might occur without people realising it, and that healing may come in different forms. There is no escaping the physical pain of grief. We only must look at losses amongst family and friends to realise that the physical pain is always hovering – it never truly leaves.

I remember feeling shattered when a young boy in our street died tragically while my brother and I were in the Hague, Holland. The news hit us like a ton of bricks. Damien was around the same age. He struggled to deal with the loss of his happy-go-lucky mate with a heart-of-gold. So, the pain of loss was close to home, and we now understand what his poor family went through.

The physical pain associated with Cara's loss remains, and each day brings a new memory. Still, we feel spiritually stronger and emotionally, better able to deal with her passing.

We have taken Lorna Byrne's advice and frequently reflect on any healing that takes place, trying to recognise when it happens or, if-and-when it is 'granted'.

Speaking to family and friends who were deeply affected by Cara's death, I am glad to know that it has helped some people to find purpose in their lives:

"Often healing can seem small—perhaps somebody who has been depressed for a long time smiles or laughs; maybe someone who was in a lot of physical distress feels a lot better; or maybe a mother who has been stressed out and unable to cope suddenly feels happiness and joy." (30).

We enjoyed regular music nights at home or to celebrate Irish events in Leeds and York. The craic was great, and the kids loved dressing up. Each St Patrick's Day, Faye would decorate the house in bunting and flags.

The day would start with an Irish breakfast including soda and potato bread (now a distant pipedream due to being gluten intolerant).

189

The music would commence late morning, and by early afternoon, we would be on our way to the parades. 'Lord of the Dance' (31) was one of the first songs Cara learnt and was subsequently played at her funeral.

I danced on a Friday when the sky turned black,
It's hard to dance with the devil on your back.
They buried my body, they thought I'd gone,
But I am the dance, and I still go on.

"Dance then, wherever you may be,
I am the Lord of the dance," said he,
"And I'll lead you all wherever you may be,
And I'll lead you all in the dance," said he.

They cut me down, but I leapt up high.
"I am the life that'll never never die
And I'll live in you if you'll live in me.
I am the Lord of the dance," said he.

Cara couldn't speak during the Tracheostomy days. She learnt some tips and tricks such as manipulating the Tracheostomy tube with her index finger and speaking in a croaky, comical voice. We still laugh at some of the one-liners, e.g. with her Derry and Belfast accents: *'Catch your big self on'; 'Jog you on there, Da'.*

After decannulation, she found her voice and became a little chatterbox. Cara's sweet voice often pierced the morning silence, and she continued to sing and play until bedtime. Just to hear that beautiful angelic voice after years of silence was precious beyond belief.

She had an excellent memory and picked up lyrics like the popular traveller song 'The Big Strong Man (32)' which she often regaled with gusto. I often sang 'Song of the Wandering Aengus (33)' to her and now wish she had learnt the words and sang it back to me.

Over this past year, at a critical time in our evolution, and as the world grapples with a pandemic, we continue to witness figures from the spirit world who appear in various shapes, sizes, and contours.

There must be a connection, and we feel humbled in the knowledge from Lorna that many spirits and angels are here to observe and protect us. We have seen a range of stunning angel-type figures of different colours and sizes, alongside images of the deceased in spirit. Cara prayed to her Guardian Angel for many years:

Angel of God, My Guardian Dear,
To Whom God's Love Commits Me Here,
Ever This "Day" (or "Night" if You Say It at Bedtime),
Be at My Side,
To Light and Guard,
To Rule and Guide,
Amen (34).

We acknowledge that this is a unique story about Cara's life and the spiritual awakenings that occurred after her passing. We wish to let people make up their own minds about the spirit world and our place in the world. This book is not aimed at a specific religious group. Our friends and colleagues stem from all faiths and denominations. They have tried to help us to make sense of the pictures and images shared since Cara died.

Certain things are mostly private to us – such as the sight of angels in their harmonious flow. Still, many of the souls and spirits have been witnessed and captured in different states. We now understand what Lorna Byrne says in her beautiful and uplifting narratives about angels (35).

They always surround us and by simply asking, we can touch base with a realm that often seems beyond our imaginations. We like the fact that Lorna Byrne refers to Gods unconditional love and the pure caring and considerate role of our Guardian Angels.

When reading through her books this past year, we cannot help but reflect on the way that the angels would chat to Lorna. They play a central role supporting, guiding, and navigating people through the tough times in their lives.

Regardless of the physical pain, which is always present, we have generated an abundance of spiritual and emotional strength and are glad to share the details of Cara's life in this way.

Cara Appears To Granny Marie

Early morning of May 25th, 2020, my mother woke from a light sleep at her home in Belfast. As she turned to the side, she noticed a young girl with long dark hair walking towards the bedroom door.

Initially, thinking that it was Carla, my youngest sister, it quickly dawned that the figure was too small. Carla's hair was also short from six months of rigorous chemo.

My mum described how the young girl simply strolled gracefully away. Judging by our own experiences in Leeds, we believe that Cara may have snuggled into bed for a cuddle with her Granny Marie and was allowed to make an appearance.

My wife and I have had similar experiences in Leeds. Most activity tends to happen at night, perhaps because of Cara's sleep problems or the fact that she died in her sleep. We agree with Lorna Byrne's assertions that there are many messages to all of this.

Post-mortem Follow-Up Results

Carla received news from her Consultant in Belfast that her kidney function had improved dramatically.

She was susceptible to infections and even more-so with COVID-19 and its broader implications because her immune system was akin to an open airway. But being housebound for months was taking its toll.

After lockdown, she was glad to take short breaks outside, so her first port of call was Clonard Monastery. As she entered, she noticed a man around 50 years old, who turned to warmly greet her.

After explaining the reason for her visit, he immediately asked, 'Who?' And upon hearing the words: 'Cara Mervyn', his eyes filled with tears as he said, 'I pray for Cara Mervyn every day'. Carla wondered how he knew, and presumed that he was one of our friends.

He briefly ran to his car before returning with a gift - a small cross which Carla could either keep for herself or send to us. Carla found the experience quite surreal.

This reminded us of the day when Cara's brain tumour biopsy results came through. Donna was strolling through Clonard Monastery when she crossed paths with another stranger.

The old man remarked: 'I've been waiting for you' before handing her a small prayer card. On the drive back, Chloe switched the radio on to find a Bob Marley song playing: 'Everything is going to be alright'. They cried but also reported feeling a surge of strength.

After Cara died, my family visited Leeds. Carla decided to check on Faye after she retreated early to bed. She noticed that Faye was tucked in almost entirely and lovingly – as if someone had taken considerable time and effort. There was also a post-it-note standing upright at the end of the bed. Everything seemed pristine and untouched. As if Faye had slipped herself into a brand-new bed cover.

The same thing happened back in Belfast. At the end of May 2020, Carla woke with a strange feeling that someone was in the room. Just then, she noticed the enclosed, creaseless bed covers. Once again, it seemed someone had deliberately, and affectionately, tucked her in and checked on her as she slept. That day, my mother was sat in the living room, when a ray of light entered and flickered before the shadow of a girl with long hair stared back in the reflection.

Later, I called Carla to explain the outcome of our web-based meeting with the oncologist, neurologist, and Macmillan nurse, where we discussed the post-mortem results. As we spoke, I described to Carla how a towering figure had appeared in Cara's trampoline, staring back at me at that moment. Again, it wasn't frightening but more surreal. Carla then mentioned that in her recent dream, she heard the word 'Prayers' in a loud and peculiar voice, which made her jump. She felt the message was a powerful reminder that many souls still need prayers.

Khalid's Vision

Cara only seemed to visit family, e.g. my wife, son, and I; niece Chloe and mum - both on two occasions, and through the appearance of supernatural events around each family home.

For instance, Chloe described significant experiences when she awoke to the sight of Cara who was sat on the end of the bed. On both occasions, she wore a white dress with a white flower nestled in her dark curly hair; white shoes and was holding a tiny white purse. Chloe mentioned how Cara didn't speak, but just laughed and smiled. She also mentioned gold and white lights surrounding the room.

Khalid Mukhtar (an international businessman) was the exception. We received a call from Khalid after Lorna's first visit, in June 2020. I knew that something was amiss by the emotion in his voice, and after a few moments, he slowly described a spiritual experience with Cara.

We found the call particularly unforgettable because Cara and Khalid had never met. I supervise Khalid on his research project, but we have yet to meet physically in person.

'Some events in life have a profound effect on us and can only be described as truly life-changing. Meeting Kieran, Faye, Cara, and Finn, has been one of those experiences for me, although I have never physically met them yet.

As my research supervisor, I had to tell Kieran that I am taking a few days off because my mother had died. His response was a very professional one and full of empathy.

It is only then that Kieran also shared the sad news of his lovely daughter, Cara, passing away only a few days earlier than my mother. I attended the funeral of my mother in Pakistan and shared Kieran's family tragedy with all of my siblings.

All of us also prayed for the little girl. During my stay in Pakistan and on my return to the UK, I started feeling the pain for Kieran and Faye and the pain kept growing.

As a father myself, I continuously thought about Cara, Kieran and Faye who had become very close friends and felt as if I had lost one of my own and the pain kept growing. I had never felt this closeness to anyone and particularly people I had never met.

I remembered my late father once saying to me that the worst thing a father can experience is the death of a child. I am not sure when it began but I started feeling such closeness to Cara and the feelings I had were not just for a friend who had lost a child but also as if I had lost one of my own children. Once again, I had never experienced this before.

I started sharing my thoughts, feelings, and experiences with Kieran. Having lost a very dear friend a few months earlier in August 2019 and then dealing with my mother's death had made me very sad but above all Cara was always on my mind.

Sadly, I lost another friend in March 2020 and couldn't even attend his funeral in London because of Covid-19. All this time, thoughts of Cara, Kieran and Faye never left me. It is only during June 2020, that I had an experience that made me think that I am going through a special period in my life.

I am not even sure if I was awake or if it was just a dream when I met Cara. I don't think the vision lasted very long but I can still feel the hug and what she said to me as if it was yesterday. There are a few things that stand out.

She was continuously smiling and said to me "look after my dad" as if she was aware that her dad was in pain and required looking after. I also felt that her smile was to make sure I understand that she is in a good place.

I cried several times thinking about my vision and didn't tell anyone until I spoke with Kieran a couple of days later. As soon as Kieran picked up the phone, I had tears in my eyes and couldn't stop crying again.

I know he was crying too, and this was one of the most beautiful moments of my life. I felt so much better after sharing my vision with Kieran and ever since, the relationship between my family and his grew, several folds.

They are part of our family now and pictures of Cara and Finn are among Serra and Dan's pictures in my study.

Last but not least, Kieran had mentioned Terry during our calls several times and his death was another shock. I felt as if I had lost a very dear friend.

Sadly, I never met Terry but just knowing about him from Kieran was something very special. I know I will meet Terry, my parents and Cara one day'.

Seeking Alternative Perspectives

We discussed the experiences and shared pictures and videos with a variety of friends and colleagues. These ranged from some of the most sceptical through to the most religious people that we knew spanning all faiths and religions. It was essential to consider a range of different interpretations.

Our friend Dee mentioned how the photos and videos were the difference between perceiving something to have happened and proving it: 'The difference is, you've got the evidence'. Father Emmanuel from Nigeria simply refers to it as 'Wonderful' and 'Beautiful' and how 'Cara is truly reaching out' to us. Shelley, our friend from California, shared spiritual experiences about her grandmother. She advised us to keep an open mind and offered a professional photographic perspective.

My colleague Dr Jyoti Mishra and our friend Tony Kelly both found the pictures amazing and used the same words about Cara looking out for us. Gary Kelly believes in an afterlife and another powerful realm that we have only just touched the surface of. My brother-in-law Damo and his family often visit Clonard Monastery to pray for Cara. Damo believes that life on earth is the real purgatory.

We have tried to capture as much evidence as possible before uploading pictures and videos to the website www.ismisecara.com. Seeing things with our naked eye confirms to us that this phenomenon is real. But what is the message?

We offered one of my MBA graduates and trusted friend and colleague, Terry Boyle (RIP) the opportunity to contribute directly to the book. Terry kindly edited the first version of Is Mise Cara in June 2020:

'Finished reading the book and it is unforgettable and didn't want to disturb your work - It's great the way it is. I'm feeling quite uncomfortable about adding my bit to your story. It is Your Story. The story of Amy Lyn's [Terry's daughter] passing, although also complex, bears no resemblance to Cara's, except for the end result and surrounding feelings, and would just detract from Cara's' [Terry Boyle, RIP 2020].

I encountered other remarkable students during my postgraduate teaching in global classrooms. Many of the students participated in webinars and web-based meetings from opulent surroundings in Australia or the Middle East to less fortunate students in favelas in Brazil or shanty towns in Africa. From extremely wealthy businessmen to child soldiers in Liberia.

One particular student was Harigo Andri from the 'Salvation Ministry Africa' who is involved with a network of churches in Madagascar. We kept in touch after his studies ended, and I often sought his advice about the paranormal and supernatural experiences. On 29.9.2020, he wrote:

'Dear Dr Kieran, I trust you are well together with your wife and Finn, your son. To begin with, I still reiterate my apology for the delay of my input regarding the supernatural phenomenon that has been occurred after the passing of your beautiful little daughter Cara. It was painful to me when you shared with me the sad news (Divine Epistle of Romans 12:15, NKjv).

I know how it feels like to have lost a beloved one. A few years ago, I lost my father and then my two brothers. If God was not there to sustain us as a family during and after the loss (Joshua 1:5b), then we don't know what would tragically happen to us. The same thing happened to you as well, and I know God was there for you during and after the passing of little Cara (Hebrew 13:5b). You are a holy family. God loves your family, and supernatural phenomenon also occurs still. If you don't mind Dr Kieran, please allow me to briefly share with you my family story back home.

I grew up in a Christian family home. Basically, we go to church every week (Hebrew 10:25). My parents believed in life after death. My mother and father used to see their respective late parents appearing to them in the form of ghosts. Sometimes this happened to them in their dreams, or they physically saw the spirit with their own eyes. The ghost appearance often talked to them and encouraged them to accomplish something. Or told them about some event due to happen for my family and they often believed it when they seen it happen under their own eyes (1Samuel 28: 3-15).

Almost every four or five years, the ghosts appeared to one or to both of my parents and told them to exhume their dead bodies (grandparents). My parents practically obeyed accordingly; otherwise, something terrible would happen like a death in our family. Their ghosts also talked about something good that will happen for my family and to believe when good things happened. This phenomenon was repeated to my parents many times before they submitted to the exhumations due to their fears and beliefs.

Consequently, we used to organize the celebration and invited people and family to partake to this exhumation party where a big feast would take place. Some people accepted the invite, and some would not according to their belief or faith. As a kid, I was scared to death if someday I'd come across my late grandparents in the form of a ghost or something. Can you imagine how panicked I was? I always lived in that fear and anguish till I reached the age of 18 from which I started to read the bible that I believed is the word of God. It took me years to finish reading the bible. I came across verses explaining about life after death in any kind of form. I would now like to share with you my opinion and input to the supernatural phenomenon that is repeatedly occurring with you. So this is what I found out:

> *- Life came from God (Genesis 2:7) - it says that God breathed into man's nostrils the breath of life and man became a living being;*
> *- And death (Ecclesiast 12: 7) is when we return to the earth which we came from, and the spirit or our breath will return to God who gave it to us as mentioned above.*
> *- When someone dies (Ecclesiast 9: 5-6) they know nothing, they have no more reward, for the memory of them is forgotten. Their hatred and their envy have now perished, nevermore will they have a share in anything done under the sun.*

Dr Kieran, I know little Cara is so dear to you, and you loved her so much. I also loved my dear dad. I loved my two brothers, but according to this impressive write-up of Ecclesiast, I totally got struck. Someone also preached about something else, 'Hope'. He said we should have hope because one day we will physically meet up again with our loved ones who slept in the dust of the earth when Jesus comes back again. This was preached during the funeral of my father, and the same one was preached in my brothers' funerals. It really encouraged and inspired me

(1 Thessalonians 4: 13-18 but we would not have you ignorant, brethren, concerning them that fall asleep; that ye sorrow not, even as the rest, who have no hope. For if we believe that Jesus died and rose again, even so, them also that are fallen asleep in Jesus will God bring with him. For this, we say unto you by the word of the Lord, that we that are alive that are left unto the coming of the Lord shall in no wise precede them that are fallen asleep.

For the Lord, himself shall descend from heaven, with a shout, with the voice of the archangel, and with the trump of God: and the dead in Christ shall rise first; then we that are alive, that are left, shall together with them be caught up in the clouds, to meet the Lord in the air: and so shall we ever be with the Lord. Wherefore comfort one another with these words.)

I also encountered another fact according to the book of Deuteronomy (18: 10-11). God forbids us to interact with the dead or call upon the dead regardless of who it is. This actually happened to my parents and some of my extended family. It also happened to Saul and Samuel as described in the above story. It happened to many other people in this world. This is very dangerous to our souls, sometimes Satan disguises himself in the appearance of an angel of light (2 Corinthians 11: 14), and he was the one concealing in the appearance of my grandparents to my parents and to others.

In my opinion, I think that the phenomenon that has been taking place at your place after Cara's death should be studied with care. It should be studied in line with the principles and bible guidelines. You and your family love God so much. If you may please pray and ask him earnestly to guide you through this process in addition to your daily experience with his holy words.

May our Lord God bless you and give you more lights on your journey to finish your book. Thanks again for being a good mentor and friend to me. This is what I could share with you Dr! If you need something, I can help with please don't hesitate to reach me out" (Harigo).

Another ex-student and good friend from Jamaica who now lives in Ireland, has also been a great source of wisdom. Rohan wrote:

"Kieran, thanks for this one. This student [Harigo] makes a lot of sense, and all pointers in this message are to be carefully considered.

The bible has been an effective map for many years, guiding humans from all walks of life. I believe the devil is the greatest master of disguise as your student accurately points out. Those images are showing up now for some time in the strangest way, but so far as you have mentioned, they seem to be harmless.

Just carefully watch the energy flow in and around the house as you have been doing. We know that both the good and dark forces can lurk in the same space. If Cara is present, she could also be accompanied by other entities. She could be keeping a watchful eye on everyone and can't move on properly. Any dreams or visions should be noted as sometimes they are more than just dreams. If at all you feel anything out of place, then maybe a different kind of clearance will be required.

There is a time and place for everything, and perhaps soon, you will have to go all out and clear the environment".

A third student (Benjamin Samuel from Nigeria) offered his perspective.

> *"For starters, it means there is an important message from Cara. Usually it will be associated with an Omen.*
>
> *For instance, when my dad died, my mum always had dreams of him visiting her, with his wedding suit and all that, and always asking her to come with him. She often confessed that to me. I always encouraged her against it though.*
>
> *Finally, she followed him after 5 years...she was buried in her wedding gown. You might not find this interesting, but then that's how we interpret this...seeing the dead even in dreams is a thing of worry for us. It is usually backed up with intensive and aggressive prayers.*
>
> *My older sister and brother have witnessed physical spiritual assault from seeing my late dad and uncle in their dreams.*
>
> *It is believed evil can adopt their faces (of the dead) to perpetrate heinous acts".*

Chinese Farmer

'I have also looked at the amazing photos and videos. How awe-inspiring! You are clearly feeling Cara's presence very closely which must be lovely for you both' (Dr Sue Picton).

The fable of the Chinese farmer helped us to put Cara's life and death into context. Time spent at home during lockdown gave us space to reminisce and relive Cara's life and to share the post-death experiences. The essence of the fable has shown us that things may not have happened as expected. But the new and emerging events over recent times have made us more philosophical about life and enabled us to laugh and live again.

For instance, the visitors have shown us that there is an afterlife. We are moving beyond the depression and sadness of Cara's passing by celebrating God's gift of lifting her from future pain.

Although not masters of our destiny, we can still control our thoughts and responses to adverse events. Cara's multidisciplinary team, including oncologist and neurologist, told us the consequences of surgery if it had happened as planned in January 2020.

She may have perished in theatre or survived but had the Tracheostomy tube reinserted. Other potentialities included physical disability and blindness or faced crippling chemotherapy and radiation, which would have had a tremendous effect on her already compromised lungs and airway.

We had one final meeting with John Goodden (neurologist), and Dr Sue Picton (Oncologist) and Carole Appleby in May 2020. John reflected on children in a similar situation under COVID restrictions at the hospital:

'Cara had a great life, fantastic holidays, and was deeply loved. If you were saying goodbye now, only one of you could visit her in intensive care to share final moments. The fact that she had an Indian meal just a few hours before and then passed in her sleep was amazing: "WOW! what a way to go '.

We agree, and rather than viewing Cara's death as a disaster, we try to simply accept it as part of life. But we understand that families perceive death in different ways, depending on the context. Anne Archer, the mother of our friend Nicki in Belfast, was diagnosed with Covid-19 during 2020. Doctors decided not to ventilate because of early-stage Alzheimer's.

The family remain bewildered about the factors leading to their mother's death and the harsh way in which their mother left this earth. For us both, the pain of loss remains. Yet, the orbs, visitors and souls signify that something magical might be just around the corner if we only open our eyes to the possibility. We close the story of Cara's life with recent words from her Neurosurgeon John:

'We thank you for the lovely email and the lovely story. Very very touching, and yes it brought a tear to my eye. As a Christian, I know I am here at God's calling to do His will to the best of my ability. Whilst some neurosurgeons may feel their "trade" proves that God doesn't exist, I feel that it proves the opposite - how this blancmange-like collection of nerves gives us life and soul and rational thought is positive proof of the existence of God in my view. I am so so pleased to see your faith coming through this book about Cara and a lovely story about her life...

Cara was a truly lovely girl. Whilst it is a tragedy that she is no longer with us, I have no doubt whatsoever that she has chosen a better place instead of this fallen and Covid-ridden world. Our eternal father has her safe and secure. For that we should be thankful however sad we are at the same time'.

Telepathic 'Dreams'

Certain lyrics have a profound effect on us all. Planxty/Andy Irvine's West Coast of Clare[i] and John O'Dreams[ii] (initially written by Bill Caddick using a tune by Tchaikovsky) were family favourites. According to European folklore, the Sandman in John O'Dreams sprinkles magical sand into the eyes of children to help them sleep.

When midnight comes, and people homeward tread; seek now your blanket and your feather bed.

Home comes the rover his journeys over; yield up the night time to old John O'Dreams.

Across the hills, the sun has gone astray; tomorrow's cares are many dreams away.

The stars are flying your candle is dying; yield up the darkness to old John O'Dreams.

Both man and master in the night are one; all things are equal when the day is done.

The prince and the ploughman, the slave and the freeman; all find their comfort in old John O'Dreams.

When sleep it comes the dreams come running clear; the hawks of morning cannot reach you here.

Sleep is a river, flow on forever; and for your boatman choose old John O'Dreams.

These hauntingly beautiful lyrics helped us to contemplate Cara's time on this earth.

Cara Guiding Us

One night, we just lay in bed watching the blue dazzle dust sparkle in the space above before we drifted to sleep. Later, I emerged from an uneasy dream with an electric-like current running through my veins.

I saw that Faye was sound asleep. But where was Finn? After lifting a pillow, my heart sank to see him lying face down.

Spinning him around, the relief of hearing him breathe was an understatement. Memories of Cara came flooding back, as I lay down and tried meditative breathing before drifting off to sleep again.

My brother introduced me to the Wimm Hoff[i] breathing method which has proven health benefits when used in conjunction with ice-cold showers. Cold showers, especially during Autumn and Winter sound ridiculous, but definitely work.

Later, that same night, Cara appeared in my dream, dressed in a pair of red and checked patterned onesie type pyjamas. We stood side-by-side, watching the faces of lost souls and grizzly appearances on the walls of our home.

Her demeanour was quite serious, instructing and then observing me pray as each image appeared and then disappeared.

She then requested a snack and stood with me in the kitchen as I made her buttery toast. Gazing at me, she then giggled before disappearing into thin air.

I awoke from the dream, wondering if she was showing me the power of prayer to counter the dark side, yet simultaneously, showing that she was at peace in the spirit world. Rather than clairvoyant dreams, mine seem to be more telepathic. I frequently seem to communicate with Cara through unconscious states.

Many profound conversations have taken place, which is of course, bizarre. Nothing like this occurred before she died. A vivid series of dreams happened when we stayed overnight in Manchester during September 2020 while Finn stayed with his grandparents.

Machu Picchu Dream

Faye and I were on a plane going up through a Peruvian ravine. The sky was beautiful, but we gradually appeared too close to the cliffs edge for comfort. After a close shave with death, we were up and flying over the lovely lush landscape.

Seconds later, we dropped from the sky while inside our jeep. Faye was at the wheel with me in the passenger seat as we landed safely but awkwardly onto a long empty motorway. We appeared to race at a risky speed before I shouted: 'slow down, or the car will flip'.

A moment later (in the dream), Faye and I tried to enter a large classroom. We were soon ushered back outside by people gathered in quiet conversation. Next, we were directed into a small space – like a crowded waiting room, packed full of miniature cereal boxes in clear containers and bottles of wine.

I asked an older man why he was drinking such expensive wine when a cheaper bottle would have been just as nice. It was then that I noticed that Cara, who seemed about seven years old, was stood between us.

Faye shouted excitedly, 'look at the orbs' as dozens of transparent spheric objects floated around the room. Cara was struggling to see them before I pointed to the other side of the room, telling her to look at them orbs dancing on the ladies' face. We then found ourselves back in the magic of Peru.

Here we were, standing on a hazardous path with a few feet to spare and a significant drop beneath. On the trail were holy looking figures with grey beards and brown smocks, selling fruit and vegetables from a stall.

I approached and asked for an apple before taking a bite. Offering him a golden coin, he politely refused by shaking his head. Smiling, he then pointed up the mountainside towards the sky. I could see an array of colours and an abundance of plantation and fruit trees. He seemed to suggest that we wouldn't need money in such a place.

We quickly returned to the small waiting room with Cara. After kisses and hugs, I remember feeling miserable about leaving her. She appeared translucent, glowing beautifully and peacefully, yet not smiling. Gazing at me, she then said:

'Dad, you need to tell my friends about this place. Tell Sarah-Jane how beautiful it is over here. You must show them, teach them about this place'.

Then she was gone. I awoke feeling content and at peace but also determined to decipher the meaning of these messages. They seemed much more than a dream, more like telepathic experiences.

Kind Lady from Beechmount

I had another vivid dream in the early hours of Sunday morning, 10.10.2020. This time, Faye, Finn, Cara and I left the Royal Victoria Hospital (RVH) in Belfast.

We walked across to an Italian ice cream shop next to St Paul's chapel - the site of Cara's Holy Communion.

The shop was different from how I remembered it. When we approached the counter, a local lady from Beechmount appeared smiling.

She was just as I had remembered her as a kid - funny and kind. In the dream, I asked for two pokes (ice cream), but she refused to take the money. After serving, I told her about the orbs and ghosts that were appearing around our home.

She put her elbows on the counter, nodded, smiled and remarked that she had: 'heard all about it'. Off she went into the side room behind the counter.

Next day, I remembered how she had died of a brain disease many years ago and left a large family behind. It seemed so surreal to dream of her after all of these years.

Terry's Boyle

Another vivid dream occurred just a few nights later. Terry had just passed away, and in my dream, Faye and I were upstairs in our old flat, preparing to visit him.

After packing a bag, we strolled down stairs, guided by a large bright orb. We watched as it moved impressively before an almighty bang woke me from my sleep. It seemed like a spiritual message from the other side.

Another night, another dream about Terry. Before going to bed, I prayed and asked Cara and Terry for a sign that they were OK. In the dream, Faye and I visited Terry in a posh hospital setting.

Faye stood at the top of his bed and me by his side. We could feel the warmth of his body heat and observed his chest rise and fall. His face appeared pinkish and healthy as he slept.

Faye looked at me and smiled, whispering 'Terry's at peace; he looks so peaceful'. I nodded and then awoke, feeling calm and serene.

Wine Dream

The following week, I dreamt again about an aeroplane taking off over a choppy sea. Looking down beneath an opaque glass-bottom flooring, we observed the massive waves breaking. Next to me was a small box with four bottles of red wine which I didn't think much about at that time. Next day, Khalid texted and asked if we liked wine and offered to send some to try.

Two days later, a parcel arrived at our home. I called Faye and asked her to guess what was in the box? 'Four bottles of red wine'. Another coincidence?

Glowing Boxes

We were reluctant to share our family dreams in this book. Yet, their frequency, depth and intensity suggest an interconnection with the supernatural and paranormal experiences that were happening daily.

I discussed my dream of glowing boxes and Archangels during our first meeting with Lorna Byrne. Late November 2020, Faye also dreamt of Lorna holding a glowing, closed box.

After asking what was in the box, Faye's morning alarm beeped and woke her up before Lorna could answer. My sister Carla had another similar dream earlier this year:

> Big mansion, me and Faye were dressed up, and Cara was holding two bright pink glitter boxes. Cara warned that we could not open the boxes yet as they weren't ready to be opened, but were made outa pure love. Then Cara told me that she had to leave and that her Da was her taxi driver. We went down a bright hallway to wave her goodbye. Down the steps she went as you [Kieran] were waiting in the car. A very powerful dream that was. [Carla Mervyn]

On another night in November 2020, we noticed that Finn was talking to Cara in his sleep. I heard the word Cara but not much else. Faye remarked how she also heard Finn talk to Cara that night in his sleep.

A few nights later, in another dream, I was in a large grey panelled and unlit room. Someone was next to me, but I couldn't identify the face.

After a short while, a small clear box window opened from knee height to the ground. I kneeled and peered through the window at this fantastic variety of colours.

Cara was standing there, appearing around five years old. Her face was glowing almost as red as her jumper, and with the most beautiful smile, she stretched out her hand. As our hands briefly touched, she said: 'I'm your friend'.

These dreams feel like vivid, real-life experiences packed full of specifics, much unlike my usual dream patterns before December 2019 which I rarely remembered.

The next flurry of dreams relates to many of the other experiences which are quite telepathic in nature. A message from Khalid arrived after returning to Leeds from Manchester, and we were amazed at the coincidences about the plane and wine.

Message trail between Kieran and Khalid

Dear brother, a couple of nights ago, I woke up around 2am and felt that someone was looking at me. As you know, I am alone in the house (they [wife and family] are still in Turkey).

The window was slightly open, and a very strong light was coming in. I looked at the source, and it looked like a plane very far away, but then it was still there half an hour later (I am not sure what I did in that half hour and why I was awake).

It looked like a star, but the light was so bright. I took a picture, and then I thought about Cara and prayed for her. [Khalid Mukhtar]

That is so surreal. I will tell you about my dream of Peru soon. Just two nights ago too, and it involved a plane [Kieran]

How interesting that you were on a plane in your dream and I was looking at the light thinking it might be a plane. This all may be a coincidence, but I think it is way more than just that. We need to continue to pray for Cara and Terry [Khalid]

This is too much of a coincidence. I never wake up ever like this in the middle of the night. And it was so beautiful and peaceful to look outside the window that it kept me awake (semi-awake) for at least half an hour. I couldn't agree more. The world needs to change. Sadly, it has become so selfish and me myself and I. I still can't believe I was woken up by this beautiful and peaceful light. God help us all and keep us on the right path. Please pass on my love to your and Terry's family. Khalid.

Cara's Ashes In Majorca

Trips to the Balearic Islands resumed in August 2020. We considered Lorna's advice to grasp every opportunity for family time and booked flights to Majorca.

Cala D'or would have been too emotional without Cara, so we stayed in Palma Nova. We tried to keep Finn occupied on the plane, but he seemed a bit lost without his buddy Cara. They travelled everywhere together.

During the flight, Faye alerted us to something outside her small window. An orb of approximately six foot in circumference was aligned to the wing, like a jellyfish with layers of spectacularly coloured circles.

I tried to snap the full image but wasn't quick enough and only managed to capture a small segment (Exhibit L, www.ismisecara.com). We felt Cara's presence from that moment and throughout the trip.

Towards the end of the holiday, we found a small secluded beach. Here, some of Cara's ashes were placed inside a Celtic cross and squeezed between rocks, a few feet above the waves.

We then scattered ashes around the sea in remembrance of Cara and the island that she loved.

Once again, the energy was incredible as the orbs and dazzle dust appeared around us. It was a magical sight. We were happy to leave a little bit of Cara by the sea.

The Exorcism

Our dreams have a definite pattern. They tend to reflect our practical, conscious experiences, e.g. Cara showing us how to manage the negative images around the home. Next day, the images may be staring at us, head on. Everywhere and anywhere, e.g. in the supermarket or on long walks through the woods.

One of my most intensive 'dreams' was of a holy woman, who I believe to be Our Lady - Mary, Mother of Jesus, the Veneration of Mary in the Catholic Church. Faye and I were sat on the sofa, when a white translucent image appeared beside the door, before slowly gliding up the living room. With feet off the floor, the large and strikingly magnificent appearance travelled towards us as we watched in silence. Opening my eyes and feeling bewildered but enchanted, I began to say the rosary.

Back to reality! Father Emmanuel received the latest batch of photographs and videos sent over the summer and kindly agreed (on 23.8.2020) to bless the house. He arrived on a wet evening in good form, which helped to ease the tension because the images were appearing more unusual and worrying.

After joking with Finn, he sat on the sofa next to the front window. Faye and I sat on the second sofa, further up the room. We talked about life after Cara and how things had changed since he last visited, some months earlier. He was intrigued by events and listened carefully and silently to our concerns.

223

After a few minutes of chatting, the first ghost-like figure [similar to Exhibit M on www.ismisecara.com] appeared next to the living room and front room doors of our home. Slightly taller than Finn, and just pure glow – it slowly drifted up the living room before disappearing into thin air.

A moment later, another figure slowly drifted up and passed the feet of Father Emmanuel towards me before disappearing. At this point, I mentioned the spirit and how this was the second time that it passed us.

Father Emmanuel's response was composed. He advised that it was OK – 'nothing to worry about'. That Cara was letting us know that she had served God's purpose on earth and was now very happy – and wants us to be assured. Over the next 45 minutes or so, the figures flowed by multiple times. Faye also witnessed orbs and flickers around the space where we congregated.

At one stage, Finn was standing next to us. When he moved position, the glowing image of a spirit took his place. It seemed to have infiltrated his body. Later, one of the figures drifted up the room as before, but this time came straight towards me. I simply opened my arms to welcome and embrace what I believed was Cara.

Two of the figures seemed about 10 feet tall. They flowed in horizontally over the priest's head - both unusually large white figures. I felt that Cara was letting us know that she was delighted to have the priest here and that the house also needed a blessing. The priest described feeling a positive energy at our home. He suggested that if Cara wasn't in a beautiful place, we would soon feel it.

We then gathered around the large table where Cara often sat watching television, and the place where the orbs started to appear. The priest didn't call it an exorcism, but it was clearly a series of blessings to drive negative souls from the house. Upon request, we provided salt and water.

He then asked for quiet and began to pray, but Finn had other ideas. The television volume went sky high and tantrums kicked in as he started crying and acting strange. Shouting and playing up.

Again, maybe someone somewhere didn't appreciate the prayers and blessings and seemed to have been up to mischief because Finn is usually a relaxed and funny child.

Thankfully, he calmed down as we followed Father Emmanuel around each room of the house as he prayed and sprayed holy water.

Afterwards, he skipped down the stairs in playful mode. He joked with Finn before suggesting that we share some of the books when published with Cara and Finn's school and to provide him with a copy. Faye and I were delighted to finally have the house blessed.

Next day, I approached Father Emmanuel and asked him to review this interpretation of his visit to our home and to verify the supernatural phenomenon that occurred. He responded:

'Good evening Kieran. That's a beautiful write-up. You are a good writer. You put everything so well. I will be happy to get a copy when published'.

It gives me goosebumps to know that my dream of Our Lady also seemed to be a premonition. The spirits that appeared to us as we spoke to Father Emmanuel resembled the beautiful figure that appeared in my dream.

Terry Boyle (RIP)

Ar dheis Dé go raibh a anam ("May his soul be at the right side of God".)

I was informed by Mitch Boyle on August 28th, 2020 (Terry Boyle's son), that his Dad was unwell in the hospital. The medical staff were curious about the last time I'd heard from him. He was found unconscious but apparently, 'his heart was fine' and he was still breathing. I explained how he'd last contacted me the previous Wednesday at 4.30pm UK time with the message:

> 'No rush on this end – I've had something 'intestinal' going on for the past week which seems to be clearing up. Was unable to attend my [Parkinson's Disease] exercise class this morning because of it. No temperature, though. I'd be very surprised if it was the dreaded virus because I've been so careful.'

I reminded Mitch to keep the faith because Terry was a tough character, but he responded some hours later that this would be his Dad's last battle.

> 'He'd been made as comfortable as possible ", but he won't be pulling through this one. He had a massive haemorrhage in his brain that the medical team deemed inoperable. He'll be moved into palliative care as soon as there is a bed available. Unfortunately, the only update will be when he passes, and that could be in a few hours, a few days, we don't know. We just don't want him to suffer'.

227

My family were shocked to hear the news but convinced that Terry would somehow make a recovery and live to fight another day. Things progressed rapidly, and Mitch prayed Lorna Byrne's 'Prayer to the Healing Angels' in Terry's ear and shared a private message as the last request from us.

'Prayer of thy healing angels

That is carried from God by Michael:

Thy Archangel pour out, thy healing Angels, thy heavenly host upon me, and upon those that I love, let me feel the beam of thy healing Angels upon me, the light of your healing hands. I will let thy healing begin, whatever way God grants it, Amen.'

? Lorna Byrne, A Message of Hope from the Angels.' (36)

Later, Mitch mentioned:

> 'No change today in Dad's status. He's tough. He's really tough. He always used to [say] that he was "...going to live to be 84 and be really nervous about it when I'm 83.....". Elissa [Terry's daughter] and I and the nursing team are now making a point to exclaim from time to time: "You made it! 84! What a great age!" He's 77, but if the tiniest part of him thinks he's 84, I think we can all call it a win. I passed along your words and prayer to him today'.

On 1.9.2020, we sent a message to Mitch to explain his Dad's influence on our family. Terry guided us through the loss of Cara and the paranormal and supernatural issues that emerged. How 'his words and advice were truly insightful and powerful, and he removed many of our worries about the souls and visitors to our home. We're forever grateful'. Mitch responded with the news:

'Dad passed away a few hours ago in palliative care at Oakville Trafalgar Memorial Hospital. Elissa was with him, and she told me that he passed very peacefully. I miss him already'.

Faye and I couldn't believe the news. Terry was a dedicated friend and spiritual guide. We had so much to look forward to. He had just agreed to collaborate on a project with me and Khalid's close friend, Naqi Azam (an international business associate and University VC Advisor) (37). Terry co-authored academic publications with Dr Nii Amoo, Becky Malby. and I. We also have research papers at different levels of development. I plan to complete these in memory of the great man himself.

Lorna Byrne's Second Meeting

Faye's birthday was approaching, so I decided to write her a birthday card from 'Cara'. Sat in my office, I was determined to let the pen do the talking – thinking of Cara and what she would be thinking. Feeling choked, I couldn't get past the first few words. My attention then turned to a tiny orb which was dancing playfully around my hand.

A bright light but no bigger than a pinhead. It moved graciously around my thumb and index finger as I slowly scribbled the message. Feeling Cara's presence, I laughed, knowing that she wasn't prepared to miss her mum's birthday.

Faye and I discussed Cara's mad shopping trips with her Granny Marie and how she loved visiting her Grandad Paddy in Ireland. My dad missed seeing Cara and Finn and offered to pay the cost of flights on several occasions during 2019. He was unable to travel to Leeds because of mobility problems. When Cara died, he mentioned how his biggest regret was not seeing the cousins all play together again in Ballycastle.

A few days after Faye's birthday, I decided to check with the Coroner again on October 2020, to determine the possibility of COVID being a factor in Cara's death. COVID swab testing was not in place at the time of her passing because 'The disease had only been discovered in China'. I suppose we'll never know. But one thing we do know, is that Cara isn't far away.

The energy at home was incredible in anticipation of our web-based meeting with Lorna on Thursday, October 8th, 2020. After further technical glitches, we managed to meet again for an hour.

This was a follow-up to our initial meeting when Cara asked Lorna to bring a message from the spirit world.

Lorna began the meeting by explaining her interpretation of the pictures and images that we had shared via Pearl's WhatsApp account.

She explained that some of the photos could be fragments of light bouncing off the dust or insects caught on camera. Others may be faces already drawn on walls and painted over, so we should keep an open mind to these experiences.

For a moment, we felt slightly disheartened that Lorna might disagree with what we saw but quickly allayed our fears by discussing the visits in more detail.

Lorna explained how this was a common theme in previous conversations with parents who had lost a child. Because we were grieving, we were simultaneously opening ourselves up to higher vibrational energy.

We were noticing details that others might not witness. Some of the images might also be the faces of animals and bugs – with their faces enlarged and appearing more vivid.

It is not always in human form. Since we were opening ourselves up to nature, we are starting to see things that others may not see.

For instance, she explained how images might appear on a tree or flowers appearing incredibly vivid in colour.

The photos that we sent to Pearl reflected the essence of nature, and by opening ourselves up to the bigger picture, we tend to see things differently, particularly when grieving.

Faye mentioned how when she enters Cara's room to pray, things like sparkles, a pale golden orb or a white feather may appear.

Apparently, this was Cara's unique way of assuring us that she was safe and sound.

We were also amazed to hear that Cara was permitted to stay and guide us through the grief longer than was usually expected.

Because Cara's soul was so pure, the purest souls do not hang around so long, but she stayed with us much longer than she should have done.

Maybe this explains why the physical experiences of Cara herself seem to have (largely) disappeared in recent months? Some sporadic visits occurred in November 2020.

It was a relief to know that Cara was still around and always will be, because of the strong bond of love between us as a family.

We were delighted to hear that Cara had finally moved on but still frequents our home and will always give us signs. She would be 'here with us now' in the meeting and knows that the conversation is about her.

Lorna continued to explain the visits from the spirit world in more detail and why they were much more frequent and vivid in the immediate months after Cara's death.

It was because Cara was 'perfect' and very close to God. The fact that she was born at 29 weeks, ill throughout her childhood and culminating in a brainstem tumour put her in an extraordinary place in the afterlife.

This possibly explains why Cara appeared to people on several occasions.

Lorna was informed about Khalid's mother passing away. How his family wept for Cara amidst their own grief. At the same time, Cara was just a child with her life ahead of her. Lorna appreciated Khalid's story.

We discussed her belief in the universality of religion and the fact that religion does not define souls.

She explained how God loves everyone and how Cara's death had a deeper purpose of helping Khalid and his family by allowing them to cry and grieve for their loss.

She described how Cara had created space for Khalid to grieve for his mother.

We further discussed the dark side, but she told us how she prefers not to give 'him' any attention.

She knows that evil is always around, but to remember that 'he' cannot physically harm us and that our faith is strong. The light still beats the darkness.

I told Lorna my dream from a few days earlier. Faye, Finn and I were sat on a low backed sofa when a bald man in a suit and chiselled chin appeared, smiling and calling my name. At first, I thought it was one of my students. Still, as he approached me, an unbelievable force of energy propelled me towards him – literally lifting me off my feet as I began to pray.

It disappeared, and as I opened my eyes, I lay in bed, knowing in my heart that it was the devil. As I lay there, I felt energy above my head before what seemed like a freezer door opening. A swirling cold breeze descended around my body, as Faye and Finn slept soundly next to me. I felt that it was the angels protecting me. Faye also experienced sinister energy the night before Lorna's meeting and prayed through the experience.

Lorna explained that the good and positive energies are Cara reaching out and guiding us. We mentioned Father Emmanuel's visit and how he was very supportive after the experience at our home. We were advised to keep the priest updated and involved. Lorna has experienced mixed levels of support from priests over the years because of their contrasting interpretations of the spirit world.

She thought that it was lovely that the priest wants us to share the story of Cara's life by bringing copies to the church and providing some books to the school.

I explained my dream of Machu Picchu and how Cara asked me to tell her friends, especially Sarah-Jane, to experience this place. At first, it seemed like I was suggesting the potential of her friends leaving the physical world.

Still, I quickly clarified to say that I thought that Cara was asking her friends 'not to be afraid'; to be kind to one another and to keep the faith. That there is an afterlife and that it's exceptional.

She revealed how 'letting go', can take many years, especially for the parents of a deceased child. It took Lorna an age to re-enter a church after her husband Joe passed away. She found the memories of her loss and the sight of coffins too overwhelming.

Our prime focus of attention should be on Finn. We were advised to create quality time for our family because siblings of deceased children can often feel isolated. So, we should be making new memories while keeping Cara's memory alive.

Faye discussed how Finn had told his teachers about the angels. After finding a white feather, he remarked 'this is from my sister Cara'.

And how each day he prays to his Guardian Angel called 'Cara'. Lorna smiled and remarked how our deceased love it when we refer to them as an angel and how, when we pray for them, they pray back.

She told us that when Cara had passed, she didn't leave the world with anything but her pure soul. We can't take anything of financial value with us when we cross to the other side.

The world is far too materially focused, and this is manifested in the way we are treating each other and the environment.

Lorna explained how she has never seen hell. All souls will go to heaven as far as Lorna has been told and she has never known otherwise.

She advised that if we focus on helping just one person, then the book will be a success: 'If you can change one person's life, then you will have made a difference'.

Lorna concluded by advising us to avoid the dark side: 'Don't give it much attention. Tell it to go away and pray immediately' when evil lurks. That we are on our own remarkable journey and how we must let go and place all our energies into Finn but also to create space for ourselves.

A few weeks after Lorna's meeting, I'd another restless night. Finally, I drifted off to sleep in the early hours of Monday, October 12th, 2020.

Here I was, back with my beautiful little girl inside our home in Bramley, in the attic roof-space. We were holding hands and waiting at what seemed like traffic lights that were preventing us from crossing to the other side. I heard the words: '...going to the other side'.

Suddenly, the man in a sharp black and white suit hovered to the immediate left of me. Amidst the silence, I felt restless and uneasy next to this suspicious character with back turned slightly, just enough to block his face.

After what seemed like an age, a bright light switched on, and I started to pray once I realised that it was him again. But in an instant, he was gone. So too was Cara.

It was as if she had guided me past the danger. It took me a while to drift off again, but later in my sleep, I heard a massive bang and a man screamed 'CARA'.

Lorna previously advised that sometimes a knock during the night will be Cara saying 'it's OK'. But in this case, it didn't seem so to me.

When I previously asked Lorna if the more sinister looking images were souls needing prayers, Lorna explained how we all have a soul.

Still, it's the people in the here-and-now, the physical world who need the prayers. She advised us on a few occasions to ignore or shout 'go away' before saying a blessing when the dark side appears.

237

Kieran: Making Sense Of It All

I decided to proofread 'Is Mise Cara / I am Cara' on Sunday 11th November 2020. Later in the book, something made me re-read Harigo, Ben and Rohan's messages about their own experiences and perceptions of the spirit world. It was unnerving to think the devil can adopt faces of the dead for ulterior purposes.

Faye disliked my habit of filming the faces as they appeared. We could be out and about, in the garden or inside each room of our home. For whatever reason, we encounter things that most people may never get to witness in person. I truly believed that the more sinister faces were souls in need of prayers. Or that Cara had brought them down to planet earth for whatever reason. There were many prayers and evidence was captured on the website in an attempt to show people what we were experiencing. We know what we see, but prefer for people to make their own minds up.

For me, things fell into place like a jigsaw puzzle over a glass of red wine. I considered Faye's words and reminisced about Chris McKee and Terry Boyle's warnings: to be careful – to be aware that poltergeists can be manipulative. My sister Sarah was also concerned and often pleaded with me to stop filming. Faye and I then discussed Lorna's advice about the images and how to deal with them.

The ominous faces do not need prayers. So it's important to focus on the more powerful energies that surround us, whether at our home or beyond. Our house is an extremely peaceful and pleasant place.

We feel an incredible energy and often see orbs and translucent floating images which we believe to be the positive angels and sometimes Cara checking up on us all.

A significant event happened on the afternoon of 19.11.2020 as we took a break from writing the final pages of the book. Faye went to collect Finn from school while I made some coffee.

Going back to the large table in the dining room, a range of coloured lights shone through the patio windows which I captured on camera.

Later, when viewing the pictures, the unmistakable image of a white angel-like figure appeared beneath Cara's handprint pictures taken at the morgue (See Exhibit A on www.ismisecara.com).

The outpouring of prayers for Cara coupled with the fact that we are open to the spirit world, probably explains the appearance of the negative forces.

But we know how to deal with that now and feel an immensely powerful presence that is beyond people's comprehension.

We feel protected by something inexplainable. We are also blessed to have support from people of all religions and faiths.

A strange run of events took place after finishing a further draft of Is Mise Cara. On one occasion, Faye's hair caught fire from a candle, and I burnt my hand in the process.

Two days later, we encountered two menacing American Pitbull-type dogs which escaped from the house opposite during our morning walk. We chatted with Khalid Mukhtar who felt that the best approach was to turn these events into a positive.

Arranged through his sister, he paid for a one-month food parcel to feed four struggling families. A fantastic act of kindness. So, amidst the darkness, comes light and hope. But the mad dreams continued into December, 2020.

In one, I dreamt of throwing bricks at some sparrows congregated above us on a transparent plastic roof. One sparrow fell at my feet, seemingly dead-as-a-doornail. I sadly scooped it up and dropped it into the toilet basin. Upon flushing, the droplets of water caused its wings to flutter, so I rushed for some tissue paper in the hope of rescuing it. Seconds later, I looked down, and it was gone. Up and away, it went.

I kept my photos and videos on an old iPod classic when Cara was just born at 29 weeks and through the early years of her life. It broke after some water damage and has lay unused for over seven years now. In this other bizarre dream, I searched for and found the device and sifted through the folders before opening the first of many images.

Looking upwards, the unmistakable figure of an angel was projected onto a large screen. Then Cara appeared and prompted me to open the second photo. The screen showed the same image, as the first - but this version of the angel was glowing and shimmering brilliantly. I must repair that old iPod.

Conclusion and a Letter to Cara

Cara was 'loaned to us from God', Lorna explained, and that it was her time to go. As we concluded our second meeting, she reminded us that Cara reached out to her in the first place. It was to guide us through the grief and to advise us with the book.

We were advised to expect some negativity, particularly from non-believers and those who have experienced loss but were missing spiritual experiences.

Lorna believes that we are experiencing the spirit world because of Cara's ultra-pure spirit and the fact that we have opened ourselves up to the energies around us.

We now conclude with our message to Cara (wee Magoo):

Dear Cara, so much has happened since you arrived on planet earth. We have great memories of your release from neonatal and treasure your first St Patrick's Day celebrations.

Sorry about getting the wrong sized Ireland shirt, but you looked so cute. You were cannulated at eight months old but we know that you struggled during the 'Tracheostomy years'.

You probably won't remember, but an emergency christening was held in intensive care which still seems like yesterday. I hope you meet the children who passed away at the LGI over the years, like the little girl from Bradford and young Muhammad with the thick dark hair.

241

You were a real warrior through the years, even after the surgical procedures and many treatments. Taking you to Ireland for the first time was a beautiful experience, and we are glad that we didn't sit around and over-think things when you weren't well. We just tried to get on and make the most of precious time.

Our whole family celebrated the small wins, like the ward decannulation and when you started primary school. But as you know, life is a roller coaster, and you faced more surgery after the decannulation failed. We found some great breathing and exercise regimes, and you gave it your best shot.

The decision to wait before jumping into adoption proved to be a lucky strike as your little brother Finn (wee Maginty) arrived shortly afterwards. He adores you and loves you so much. It was the right decision to move home, and you managed to find some great friends at school, particularly your BFF Sarah-Jane :).

You and Finn's (proper) christening in Belfast was sweet, and things appeared to be finally falling into place. It all seemed too good to be true, and so it proved with your brainstem tumour diagnosis and the proceeding 18 months of worry. But we were glad to make the most of the time by organising extra holidays to Majorca and Donegal and short trips to Belfast, London and Newcastle.

Do you remember when we visited Old Trafford to watch the Manchester United legends game against Bayern Munich? Glad you enjoyed it, apart from dad embarrassing you by belting out United songs at the stadium. We know that you loved Donegal and in particular Bundoran (,e.g. Mum winning the toy dog). Still, the faith healer had some revelations for you when you arrived back in Belfast in July 2019.

We were so glad that you made it to high school and looked so grown up in your uniform. Mum misses her shopping trips with you, and all the family on both sides miss you so much.

Your last Christmas was very special, and I'm so glad your room was organised and looking beautiful with your new things. We are chuffed that your last meal was an Indian and noticed how you cleared your plate in those final hours.

Even though God called you back, we were so glad that you picked us as your parents, and hope that we did you proud. Your journey through life was unique. We know you always had to get the last word, and we know for a fact that you are still around.

Mum mentioned her recent dream, where she was reading a text message from you which said 'Mum, tell Dad that I wouldn't have coped in this world'.

You haven't left us and never will. We know that your Guardian Angel took you safely to heaven and one day, our Guardian Angels will do the same.

We will all be together again. Slan for now, Magoo. But not bye forever. Love Mum, Dad and Finn X.

About The Authors

Faye Louise Mervyn graduated with a BA Hons in Sociology from Liverpool John Moores University. She has held administrative and managerial roles and is currently Project Manager and Co-Director for Finncara Consulting Ltd. Faye has 20 years' experience and a record of working to very high standards in research and management consultancy. She excels in collaboration; and possesses a proven record of inspiring others in different working environments. Faye may be reached at ismisecara@gmail.com

Dr Kieran Patrick Mervyn is Co-Director of Finncara Consulting Ltd and Visiting Professor at London South Bank University. He is also a research and management consultant in health and social care, and an evaluation and insight analyst. Kieran has been involved in extensive research project work on Leadership and Innovation. This included working for the Northern Leadership Academy (NLA), Centre for Innovation in Health Management (CIHM) and London South Bank University (Associate), where he currently evaluates the Darzi Clinical Leadership programme and the Senior Leader Degree Apprenticeship Programme. Kieran has published widely in international journals including the Journal of the American Society for Information Science and Technology (JASIST); Information Communication and Society (ICS) and the International Journal of Leadership in Public Services (IJLPS).

Kieran may be reached at ismisecara@gmail.com / kieran@finncaraconsulting.co.uk

Kieran's Publications

Bellamy, L.C., Amoo, N., Mervyn, K. and Hiddlestone-Mumford, J., 2019. The use of strategy tools and frameworks by SMEs in the strategy formation process. International Journal of Organizational Analysis.

Mervyn, K., Amoo, N. and Malby, R., 2019. Challenges and insights in inter-organizational collaborative healthcare networks. International Journal of Organizational Analysis.

Boyle, T.J. and Mervyn, K., 2019. The making and sustaining of leaders in health care. Journal of Health Organization and Management.

Darzi Clinical Leadership Fellows: an activity theory perspective. Journal of Health Organization and Management, 2018. Vol. 32 Issue: 6, pp.793-808, https://doi.org/10.1108/JHOM-05-2018-0133 (Authors, Prof. Rebecca Malby, Dr. Kieran Mervyn, Terry J. Boyle).

Longitudinal Study of the Impact of the London Darzi Fellowship Programmes Years 1 – 8 (Jan 12, 2018) - London South Bank University (Authors: Dr Kieran Mervyn; Prof. Becky Malby).

'Types of Networks Explained' Chapter 3 in "Networks in Healthcare: Managing Complex Relationships" (2016). Emerald Group Publishing. Authors: Dr Kieran Mervyn and Prof Rebecca Malby (in Malby & Anderson-Wallace, 2016).

Innovation and Sustainability in a Large-Scale Healthcare Improvement Collaborative: Seven Propositions for Achieving System-wide Innovation and Sustainability. International Journal of Sustainable Strategic Management. 2016 Authors: Dr Kieran Mervyn, Dr Nii Amoo, Prof. Becky Malby.

Digital inclusion and social inclusion: a tale of two cities. Information, Communication & Society February 11, 2014. Authors: Dr Kieran Mervyn, David Kelvin Allen, Anoush Simon

How professionals can lead networks in the NHS. International Journal of Leadership in Public Services 2013. Authors: Dr Kieran Mervyn, Becky Malby, Luca Pirisi

Social-Spatial Context and Information Behaviour: social exclusion and the influence of mobile information technology. Journal of the American Society for Information Science and Technology (JASIST) March 1, 2012 Authors: Dr Kieran Mervyn, Dr David Allen

Challenges and Insights in Inter-Organizational Collaborative Healthcare Networks: An Empirical Case Study of a Place-Based Network BAM (2016) Conference – Full paper under the Public Management and Governance track; Amoo, Nii; Malby, Rebecca; Mervyn, Kieran

The Health Foundation's position statement on effective leadership development interventions. The Health Foundation, London 2009. Authors: Dr Kieran Mervyn, Lisa Anderson, Becky Malby, Richard Thorpe

Creating a culture of learning to drive innovation in business: Ambition Magazine Apr 2017. Author: Dr Kieran Mervyn

Networks: A briefing paper for The Health Foundation, London May 2012: Authors: Dr Kieran Mervyn, Becky Malby (Work was undertaken by CIHM, Leeds University Business School, on behalf of the Health Foundation, London)

Summary of the literature to inform the Health Foundation questions. The Health Foundation, London May 2012. Authors: Dr Kieran Mervyn, Becky Malby. Work was undertaken by CIHM, Leeds University Business School, on behalf of the Health Foundation, London

Social Networks: The Health Foundation, London May 2012. Authors: Dr Kieran Mervyn, Becky Malby. An Additional Literature Review for The Health Foundation, London, undertaken by CIHM, Leeds University Business School

The changing face of Nigerian MBA students Vanguard media limited September 22, 2014. Authors: Dr Kieran Mervyn

Are Entrepreneurs Born or Made? Entrepreneurs Middle East November 10, 2014 Authors: Dr Kieran Mervyn

Brief Literature Review on Improvement at Systems Level for the Leeds Institute for Quality Healthcare (LIQH). Prepared for The Centre for Innovation in Health Management (CIHM) - University of Leeds. August 2014. Authors: Dr Kieran Mervyn, Nii Amponsah Amoo

'Trep Toolkit': Trend Prediction 2015 - Online to Offline (O2O) Entrepreneur Middle East January 2015. Author: Dr Kieran Mervyn

How to choose an MBA; Middle East Entrepreneurs April 2015. Author: Dr Kieran Mervyn

January 2016 'Collector's Edition': Executive Summary. Entrepreneur Middle East January 2016; Author: Dr Kieran Mervyn

The Entrepreneur Middle East released it's 'Collector's Edition' in January 2016 – a standalone version of the magazine, which looks at the region's biggest enterprise influencers and issues of the past two years – and it features Kieran in its '107 Opinion Shapers of Commerce, Government and Industry'. Kieran was featured at number 87.

Project Management Insights: The Difference Between Success and Failure for SMEs GULF ELITE; July 2016; Author: Dr Kieran Mervyn.

Honours and Awards. Top 107 Opinion Shapers of Commerce, Government and Industry. The Entrepreneur Middle East. January 2016

QUOTE IN MEMORY OF "MAGOO"

I think the purest of souls, those with the most fragile of hearts, must be meant for a short life. They can't be tethered or held in your palm. Just like a sparrow, they light on your porch. Their song might be brief, but how greedy would we be to ask for more? No, you cannot keep a sparrow. You can only hope that as they fly away, they take a little bit of you with them [Emm Cole].

BIBLIOGRAPHY

1) Consulted online at: https://www.thefuneralpoem.com/10/famous-poets-poems/mary-elizabeth-frye/70/do-not-stand-at-my-grave-and-weep-death-poetry-verses?paid=28 15.11.2020

2) The Parable of the Chinese Farmer: Consulted online at: http://pediatricservices.com/prof/prof-47.htm [See also: https://www.cleveland.com/living/2009/02/parable_of_a_chinese_farmer_ho.html Consulted online at: 15.11.20203

3) Missing You written by Jimmy MacCarthy in the 1980s and popularised by Christy Moore: https://www.christymoore.com/lyrics/missing-you/

4) https://complexchild.org/articles/2012-articles/april/blood-gases/

5) https://westleedsdispatch.com/marks-history-walk-including-haunted-abbey-inn-and-secret-tunnels/

6) High school musical (2007): Kenny Ortega; Don Schain; Peter Barsocchini; Zac Efron; Vanessa Hudgens. Publisher: Burbank, California: Walt Disney Studios Home Entertainment, Burbank, California. Distributed by Buena Vista Home Entertainment. [2007] https://www.worldcat.org/title/high-school-musical-2/oclc/166353152

7) https://www.buteykobreathing.org/

8) https://www.health.harvard.edu/mind-and-mood/relaxation-techniques-breath-control-helps-quell-errant-stress-response

9) https://www.health.harvard.edu/mind-and-mood/relaxation-techniques-breath-control-helps-quell-errant-stress-response

10) Reel in the Flickering Light, by Column Gallagher. Sang by Christy Moore: https://www.youtube.com/watch?v=zWDStK5Mni0

11) https://www.nhs.uk/conditions/brain-tumours/

12) The Chapel has a carved altar with a canopied niche, gargoyles, a vaulted ceiling, roof bosses, pillars with floriate capitals, a Celtic head, a piscina and externally a large carving of a medieval knight guards the entrance.

13) http://chapelofourladyofthecrag.btck.co.uk/

14) https://www.mothershiptoninnlowbridge.co.uk/index

15)http://www.iubilaeummisericordiae.va/content/gdm/de/mondo/porte-della-misericordia.event.shrine-of-st-margaret-clitherow-diocese-of-middlesbrough.html

16) http://www.stwilfridsyork.org.uk/shrine-st-margaret-clitherow.php.

17) https://www.cardinalheenan.com/

18) Darby O'Gill and the Little People: https://www.imdb.com/title/tt0052722/ [Consulted online at: 16.11.2020].

19) Black is the Colour: https://www.youtube.com/watch?v=kzhicxPANRo

20) Anonymous (2016): https://www.houstonarchitecture.com/haif/topic/33365-a-christian-biblical-study-of-spiritual-orbs/

21) Naparstek, B. (2009) Your sixth sense: Unlocking the power of your intuition. New York: Harper Collins

22) http://ardara.ie/assaranca/

23) https://www.kingjamesbibleonline.org/Matthew-19-26/

24) Brick Johnstone, Angela Bodling, Dan Cohenb, Shawn E. Christ, & Andrew Wegrzyn (2012). Right Parietal Lobe-Related "Selflessness" as the Neuropsychological Basis of Spiritual Transcendence International Journal for the Psychology of Religion: 10.1080/10508619.2012.657524

25)https://www.patheos.com/blogs/epiphenom/2012/07/different-parts-of-the-brain-linked-to.html

26) Park, H., 2020. Neuroscience, Selflessness, and Spiritual Experience: Explaining the Science of Transcendence: by Brick Johnstone and Daniel Cohen, San Diego, CA, Academic Press, 2019, x+ 181 pp., 79.77(paperback), 94.99 (digital), ISBN 978-0-08-102218-4.

27) Lorna Byrne: www.lornabyrne.com

28) https://www.holyart.co.uk/blog/saints-and-blessed/archangels-who-are-they-and-what-is-their-function/

29) 'This Irish folk song is about the passing of a father. The song was written by By Phil Coulter and Recorded by The Fureys And Davie Arthur [songs] who sing the song in the YouTube video [see https://www.youtube.com/watch?v=JCSaBYY-wQk], also by Celtic Thunder and John McDermot. Some people call this song "My Old Man"] https://www.irish-folk-songs.com/the-old-man-lyrics-and-chords.html.

30) Lorna Byrne (2009) 'Angels in my Hair,

31) https://stainer.co.uk/Lord-of-the-dance/

32) The Big Strong Man: https://www.youtube.com/watch?v=d7yiUxCmqrI

33) Song of the Wandering Aengus WB Yeats (1987): Youtube version by Christy Moore: https://www.youtube.com/watch?v=BBPF9sJR13A

34) 'For many years it was believed that St. Anselm of Canterbury, a Benedictine monk who lived during the 11th century, was the author of the prayer. However, recent scholars have discovered that the prayer was likely inspired by Reginald of Canterbury, another Benedictine monk who lived at the same time as St. Anselm. Scholars found a prayer in Reginald's Life of St. Malchus that bears a strong resemblance to the current Angel of God prayer'. https://aleteia.org/2017/10/02/who-composed-the-angel-of-God-prayer/

35) https://www.amazon.co.uk/Lorna-Byrne/e/B002HZ0VFA

36) https://www.amazon.co.uk/Message-Hope-Angels-Sunday-Bestseller/dp/1444765779

37) Naqi is a a a banking and management professional; advisor to the Vice Chancellor in a Pakistan University and visiting adjunct faculty in Malaysia, Philippines and Cambodia.

Printed in Great Britain
by Amazon

53860279R00156